PROPHETIC PREACHING

THE PREACHER'S TOOLBOX
COMMUNICATING GOD'S WORD WITH POWER

PROPHETIC PREACHING

FRANCIS CHAN
JOHN ORTBERG
TIMOTHY KELLER
MARK BUCHANAN
ANNE GRAHAM LOTZ
MARK DRISCOLL
KENNETH ULMER
And more...

Craig Brian Larson, General Editor

HENDRICKSON
PUBLISHERS

Prophetic Preaching

Hendrickson Publishers Marketing, LLC
P. O. Box 3473
Peabody, Massachusetts 01961-3473

ISBN 978-1-59856-704-5

Printed in the United States of America

Fourth Hendrickson Edition Printing — April 2016

Library of Congress Cataloging-in-Publication Data

Prophetic preaching.
     p. cm. — (The preacher's toolbox ; bk. 1)
    ISBN 978-1-59856-704-5 (alk. paper)
    1. Preaching. 2. Prophecy—Christianity.
    BV4221.P76 2012
    251—dc23
                2011041052

TABLE OF CONTENTS

Foreword: Craig Brian Larson   vii

Introduction: Matt Woodley   1

Part 1: The Calling of Prophetic Preaching

1. The Basis of Prophetic Preaching
   Francis Chan   11

2. Preaching in the City of Man
   Mark Buchanan   19

3. Preaching Like Jesus
   James MacDonald   29

4. Grace-full Prophetic Preaching
   Bryan Loritts   41

5. Preaching Like a Prophet
   John Ortberg   47

6. What All Good Preachers Do
   Craig Brian Larson   59

7. The Clint Eastwoods of the Pulpit?
   Lee Eclov   67

8. When God Is Revealed, Knees Bow
   Mark Driscoll   75

Part 2: The Craft of Prophetic Preaching

9. A New Kind of Urban Preacher
   Timothy Keller   81

10. The Unchanging Grounds of Our Authority
    John Koessler   89

11. The Three Kinds of Preachers
    James MacDonald   101

12. Challenging Hearers
    Lyle Dorsett   105

13. Applying and Preaching from the Old Testament
    Prophets
    Andrew C. Thompson   119

14. Preaching for Revival
    Anne Graham Lotz   131

15. His Word in Your Mouth
    Kenneth Ulmer   141

FOREWORD

"Wisdom is supreme; therefore get wisdom.
Though it cost all you have, get understanding."
(Proverbs 4:7)

That verse certainly applies to preaching. As editor of PreachingToday.com since 1999, I have listened to many sermons, and it is sobering to consider how many ways preaching can go wrong, from bad theology to bad interpretation of texts, from extremes on one side to extremes on the other, from being a people pleaser to being a people abuser, from confusing hearers to boring them. If there is any group of people in dire need of wisdom, it is preachers.

We find that wisdom in Scripture in large measure, of course. But while the Bible is our all-sufficient source book for what we preach, and for the theology of preaching and the character of the preacher, it is not a preaching manual. For much of what we need to know about preaching in our generation, in our geography, we need wisdom from one another.

We need the insights of those who have preached for 50 years, who have seen fads come and go, who have made mistakes themselves, and who can keep us from repeating them. We need the new perspective of young preachers who understand where the culture is going in ways that veteran preachers may not.

We need to hear from contemporary preachers who have read the wisdom of the church collected over hundreds of years on the subjects of preaching, pastoring, the care of the soul, theology, interpretation, sermon application, human nature, communication. We need to hear the wisdom of other "tribes" within the church, for each denomination or movement develops its own way of preaching, with its particular strengths and weaknesses.

In this book series, you will find a breadth of such wisdom. Since 1999, PreachingToday.com has published articles each month from outstanding practitioners on the essentials of preaching. This series of books with Hendrickson will draw from that bank vault of wisdom, bringing you timeless wisdom for contemporary preaching with the goal of equipping you for the most important work in the world, the proclamation of the glorious gospel of our Lord Jesus Christ.

And week by week, through the ups and downs, ins and outs of their lives, your congregation will be glad they have come to the house of the Lord to hear you preach. In your voice, your flock will hear the voice of the Chief Shepherd, the Overseer of their souls.

Let it be, O Lord, by your grace!

—Craig Brian Larson, editor of PreachingToday.com

INTRODUCTION

Nobody likes to hear those dreaded words from the doctor: "You need surgery." It always comes as a shock. Many of us respond by shopping around for a second opinion, but that usually doesn't change reality: We have a problem and we need help. Someone needs to open the clogged arteries, remove the malignant tumor, repair the ligaments, or reset the broken bone.

On one level, those words often bring relief. We knew we had a problem. We knew we weren't whole. So although a negative diagnosis wasn't what we *wanted*, the doctor was telling us what we *needed* to hear. Also, we know that our doctor has one ultimate agenda: to restore our long-term health. As a result, we allow—and even expect—our trusted physicians to speak the truth into our lives, even when it's uncomfortable. Only an incompetent or uncaring doctor would avoid giving us accurate information about our health.

It's no different in our spiritual lives. We need honest, trustworthy doctors of the soul who will speak uncomfortable truths into our lives. Even after following Christ for many years, we still have hidden corners of disease—secret sins, spiritual immaturity, and unhealed wounds. As the psalmist confessed, "There is no health in my body; there is no soundness in my bones because of my sin" (Ps. 38:3). We can avoid and deny this spiritual disease for years until someone uses God's Word, not as a weapon to bludgeon us, but as a scalpel to cut through our layers of excuses and evasions. It takes courage and compassion, but these trustworthy pastors speak the truth, identifying our sin, calling it by name, and then gently leading us to the One who can heal our souls.

That summarizes the ministry of prophetic preaching. This vital practice diagnoses the disease within us. Like a good doctor, prophetic preachers don't sugarcoat the truth; they don't ignore or minimize the painful verdict; and they'll declare what we need to hear, not necessarily what we want to hear. With confidence and courage they'll say, "You have a problem. You can get a second opinion, but I'll tell you right now that there's only one treatment—the gospel. By the authority of God's Word, I can say that you need help—God's help. And by that same authority, I'm here to proclaim that in Jesus' life, death, and resurrection God is with you and for you. He is the Healer of your soul."

But prophetic preachers don't merely address individual or personal issues. At times they also must confront the broader social aspects to our spiritual unsoundness—injustice, poverty, racism, sexual immorality, and false teaching. These larger issues also rupture wholeness and degrade people who bear God's image and who are loved by Christ.

Our churches need bold, compassionate, Christ-centered, and Spirit-filled prophetic preaching. Unfortunately many preachers harbor negative attitudes toward prophetic preaching. (I know I did.) It's often viewed as a special or even odd calling that's reserved for just a few pastors. Sometimes it conjures up images of preachers who rail against contemporary culture while they make outlandish predictions about the future. Or, even more negatively, prophetic preachers sometimes get squeezed into one, narrow personality profile: they're angry, loud, tactless people who want their listeners to feel ashamed, defeated, or offended.

The pastors in this book will dismantle all of these dreary, moralistic, and unbiblical misconceptions of prophetic preaching. For starters, it's impossible to squeeze them into one personality type or even one preaching style. James MacDonald talks and thinks very differently than John Ortberg. Tim Keller's ministry in Manhattan looks very different from Bryan Loritts's multiethnic church in Memphis. Just as there wasn't one template for biblical prophets (think of the profound differences between Jeremiah, Amos, Hosea, and Jonah), so there isn't one prophetic style for today. As Bryan Loritts points out, "Whether you see yourself as a prophetic preacher or not, anyone who stands up and opens up the Bible and says, 'Here's what God says,' is really taking on the mantle of a prophet." In other words, God can use all kinds of personality types to declare his truth and confront our spiritual ailments.

But in the midst of this diversity, this book also stresses some clear themes about prophetic preaching. First, prophetic preaching always begins with a high view of Scripture. There's an assumption that God has something to say right now, in this city, to this group of people gathered for worship—young and old, rich and poor, American and Nigerian and Brazilian and Korean, believer and skeptic. God's Word is sharper than any two-edged sword; it will cut clean through us, even the deepest parts of us (Heb. 4:12). As James MacDonald argues, we should treat the Bible like a lion: just let it out of the cage, get out of the way, and it can take care of itself. So, ultimately, the authority for prophetic preaching doesn't reside in the preacher's intelligence, confidence, or cleverness—and that sure takes a load of pressure off of us as preachers. Prophetic authority flows as God's Word exposes sin, confronts strongholds in our lives, leads people to Jesus, and sets the captives free.

Second, although prophetic preaching starts with God's Word, it also flows through a preacher's heart. What's different about a prophetic preacher's heart? In chapter 1 Francis Chan calls it a "holy discontentment." It begins with a pastor who feels burdened with the things that break the heart of God. The world and individual lives are bent and twisted. Something is out of whack, and it needs to be set straight. Or as Craig Brian Larson argues, our culture has veered off course, "slogging its way through moral fog and quicksand." Most people look at this moral fog and just shrug their shoulders. But prophetic preachers get gripped by the holy love of Jesus and they can't let it go. As John Ortberg writes, "To us, the world is not so bad." But "the prophets act like the world is falling apart." Contemporary prophets weep with the heart of Jesus as they also long for Christ to come and set things right.

Third, based on this sense of holy discontentment, prophetic preachers have a sense of urgency. That doesn't imply that pastors have to act like cranks and killjoys. It doesn't mean that preachers must omit personal stories, illustrations, cultural insights, or anything remotely funny from their sermons. As Timothy Keller and John Koessler will argue, good preachers can boldly declare God's Word and winsomely engage culture. (Actually, if listeners don't connect with preachers, they'll just tune out the sermon.) But prophetic preachers also know that during each sermon human souls hang on a precipice between good and evil, God and idols, obedience and rebellion, heaven and hell. Marriages, families, and communities desperately need direction and healing. Thus the end game of preaching isn't providing information or entertainment. People (both Christians and non-Christians) need to repent, believe the gospel, grow in Christ, and serve the world.

Fourth, prophetic preachers are motivated by love for people. If preachers merely vent their anger or frustration, they won't convey God's broken heart for his wayward people. Mark Buchanan calls this "the Jonah approach"—an angry assault on everything that's wrong with the world. For some reason we think we're helping God by pressuring, threatening, and shaming people to shape up. That never works over the long haul. As Buchanan warns, "If we take the Jonah approach, we can miss the spiritual hunger that is underneath things in our culture that are deplorable on the surface."

Instead, gripped by Christ's love for lost people (or just confused and rebellious believers), prophetic preaching seeks to break and win hearts. According to Mark Driscoll, "Preaching is unique in its power to break people. And once broken, once softened, God rebuilds repentant lives." Of course, people may still walk away unbroken and unconverted, but at least they'll feel provoked, challenged, and perhaps even intrigued by God's Word and the sincere love of Christians.

Finally, prophetic preaching brings hope to the listener. Surprisingly, many people in our culture long for preachers who can humbly and confidently say, "This is what God says about ____." The tone of prophetic messages doesn't have to seep with negativity. Although it exposes the damage of sin, idolatry, or injustice, it also declares Christ's power to meet our deepest needs and transform society. Thus prophetic preaching always leads to hope: After surgery there's health; after sin there's forgiveness; after injustice there's God's shalom; after judgment there's redemption.

Clearly, prophetic preaching never throws us back on ourselves and our own resources; it always leads us to the Savior who can help us change. One of the chapters in this book quotes Charles Spurgeon, who once gave this secret to preaching: "I take my text and make a beeline for the cross." So the essence of prophetic preaching isn't "you're a mess; try harder to clean up your life." That kind of moralistic preaching doesn't help people—and it isn't the gospel of Jesus Christ. Instead, prophetic preaching says, "Yes, you are a mess (and I'm a mess and the whole world's a mess), but in Christ, you have everything you need to start life anew. Your heavenly Father is waiting to adopt you. God the Son is able to forgive and restore you. The Holy Spirit will empower you with Christ's presence."

This book is divided into two parts. Part 1, "The Calling of Prophetic Preaching," addresses the nature of prophetic preaching. What is it? What are the common misconceptions of prophetic preaching? What is the biblical basis for prophetic preaching? What's the purpose and aim of prophetic preaching? What is the "dark side" of prophetic preaching? Why is prophetic preaching important? What happens if we ignore the prophetic dimension in our preaching?

Part 2, "The Craft of Prophetic Preaching," focuses on the practical aspects of prophetic preaching. How do you do it? How do you connect with listeners, especially given our skeptical, antiauthoritarian cultural setting? How do we engage in other people's stories without diluting the story of Jesus Christ? How do we challenge but not overwhelm people with the call of discipleship? How do we take the ancient biblical prophetic texts and apply them to our setting? If prophetic preaching doesn't come naturally to us, how do we grow in this aspect of our pastoral ministry? How do we bathe our messages in prayer?

Prophetic preaching is a high and holy calling. As Kenneth Ulmer reminds us in the last chapter, for some crazy reason God has put his word in a preacher's mouth. God wants to speak his words of life through you. But, ultimately, this calling depends on God, because he's faithful and you are in his hands. So Ulmer urges us, "Thank him that he's called you to be a pastor. Thank him that he's put his words in your mouth. Thank him that the anointing of God rests in your life. Thank him that he's picked you up and turned you around. Thank him that he's placed you before his people with his word in your mouth."

— Matt Woodley

The Calling of
Prophetic Preaching

THE BASIS OF PROPHETIC PREACHING

Francis Chan

Few pastors preach with as much prophetic urgency as Francis Chan. That's why he's the "leadoff batter" for this book. But notice how clearly Chan bases prophetic preaching on God's Word—not the preacher's personality, brilliance, or effort. Having a high view of Scripture (Chan calls it a "trembling at his Word") isn't always comfortable. Submitting to God's Word will give us, like Chan, an emotionally intense "holy discontentment" for the "things that God cares about deeply." A sense of prophetic urgency will replace our casualness toward sin, brokenness, and injustice.

But Chan also humbly (and prophetically) warns us that our sense of urgency may cause us to miss the ultimate goal of prophetic preaching—love (see 1 Cor. 13:1–2). The reminder to love people will get repeated often throughout this book. It's a good litmus test of whether we're preaching as true prophets or just angry cranks. Chan has enough honesty to know when he's so driven by his own self-centered "urgency" that he offends and wounds his listeners. But as Chan also states, when we're grounded in God's Word, led by the Holy Spirit, and motivated by love, we can preach hard truths and walk in joy and confidence, even if we offend people.

The beginning of prophetic preaching

Prophetic preaching begins with something we've largely lost in the American church culture—a high view of God's Word. Very few of us tremble when we hear or read God's Word. But in my opinion that's the basis for my experience with prophetic preaching and for others who have the same gift. It's as though God screams out to us from the words of the Bible. When I want to know how the Lord wants me to share with his people, he'll make it clear to me and biblical passages will come to mind. But there are also life callings—things he's given me that I've been passionate about because of my involvement in the church.

Seven or eight years ago, the Lord opened my eyes to care for the needy all around the world. He did this through my experiences but also through Scripture. All those Bible passages about caring for the poor suddenly leaped out at me. At the same time, other Christian leaders around the United States were getting the same message from God's Word.

Then a few years ago, God started leading me to understand and emphasize the Holy Spirit. Suddenly passages about the Holy Spirit started screaming out to me from the Scriptures. I don't think it was a coincidence that at the same time many of my friends who are also church leaders started getting the same message from God and from his Word.

In the past two years, the focus of my life has shifted to what the church should look like. What type of relationships are we supposed to have with one another? I saw the stark contrast between the connection of the family of believers in the Bible and what we see today in the American church. Every time I'd read those passages, I couldn't just leave it alone. And sure enough, as I looked around, other leaders were wrestling with the same things.

In contrast, it's also clear who acts more like a false prophet. When you look at the biblical warnings about false prophets, much of it has to do with their character: their greed, lack of love, self-centeredness, and pride. That reveals their hypocrisy and their true status as false prophets. Based on these biblical warnings about false prophets, it's not surprising that Paul tells Timothy, you need to guard your life and doctrine closely.

Sadly, I've seen many people get away from the Scriptures, and I've never seen it end up with good fruit. At times I can sound like a broken record, but everything has to be centered on the Word of God. If we start getting the applause of man, we can start relying on our intellect or instinct rather than spending time in the Word. I've seen other preachers get lazy with the Word, and I can do that as well. Of course sometimes we slip into another bad habit with God's Word: We rely too much on things that God has taught us in the past, instead of studying the Word every week so we can get a fresh word from the Lord.

The Word of God and daily experience

So when it feels like God is using his Word to bring things to my attention, that's usually the first impulse for what becomes prophetic preaching. It seems like the Lord mixes his Word with my daily experience. It's so God ordained that at times I can't deny it. But I always want the Word to remain at the center of my preaching, because we can be fooled by experience. Satan is the master of deception, so we must not base our preaching on our intellect or opinion. God inclines the heart of certain men to give certain messages, but it will always be in line with the Scriptures.

Personally, Scripture-based and Scripture-centered preaching is the only kind of preaching that makes sense to me. I don't know any other way to teach. I believe the Lord gives me a message every week. It's hard for me to teach unless I believe that God has given me that message for the people. I think it is part of the gift set that God has given me. I don't know how to explain it, but I have a sense of urgency every time I teach. I really do believe my message is from God, and it is something that he's revealed to me. Not everyone takes the same approach to preaching, but it seems to be the way that God works with me.

That doesn't imply that I preach the same way every week. My preaching often follows a different pattern during particular seasons in the life of the church. For example, the other night I woke up with Ephesians 5:18–21 in my mind, especially what it means to be Spirit filled. Through circumstances and through his Word, God has been speaking to me about losing some of the joy in my ministry. Unfortunately I don't always follow the clear instructions from God about the Spirit-filled life according to Ephesians 5:18—speaking to others in psalms, hymns, spiritual songs, making a melody in my heart to the Lord, and giving thanks for everything. I need to get back to being a thankful person, giving thanks all day long, and having a melody in my heart. So that's what I'll be preaching on soon. That may not turn into a longer series. At times God will lead me to preach on a particular topic for a few weeks. At other times, he'll nudge me toward preaching an entire book in the Bible—and that's a project that could take weeks or even months to complete.

The emotions of prophetic preaching

But prophetic preaching isn't just about going through the motions of preaching about the Bible. It can also be intense and emotional. Sometimes I have a deep sadness for people who don't get it. God will give me a deep concern for people that almost feels like frustration at times. More often it feels like a holy discontentment, especially over our lack of holiness. I'm bothered when people seem apathetic about the things that God cares about deeply. Or I'm bothered that people are casual about sin. God often helps me see how serious sin is, and that gives me a real passion to live according to his Word. At other times, like leaders in the Bible, I feel a Christlike anger when people are indifferent to God's Word.

On the other hand, sometimes I feel intense joy as I'm preaching God's Word. During the act of preaching, I'm brimming with God's presence, and then when I'm done I feel like I just had an amazing devotional time with him. When we think about experiencing the Holy Spirit, we tend to think of getting away into the mountains or the beach by ourselves. But I've also known times when I'm filled with the Spirit right in the midst of teaching others. It really is a spiritual gift or a manifestation of the Spirit. Afterward I'm so grateful to God for letting me be used.

The main goal of prophetic preaching

Of course there's also a dark side or a danger in prophetic preaching: a lack of love for others. At times I'm focused on what God wants me to say, but I forget that God also wants me to love people in the process of preaching. Paul said it so clearly in 1 Corinthians 13: I can preach prophetically all day long, but if it's not done in love, it profits me nothing. I've been guilty of that kind of loveless preaching. Then there are other times when my flesh takes control, and I exude my human anger or frustration instead of the Spirit's thanksgiving and peace. So when I preach but I'm not displaying the fruit of the Spirit, I can fool myself into thinking that I nailed the passage because I proclaimed it boldly. On the other hand, I can also fail God because I let the fear of people temper what I should say about a serious topic. I try to think too much about how to say it perfectly so it doesn't offend anyone. At times I've even backed off from saying everything God wanted me to say because I was afraid of rejection. So it goes both ways.

Ultimately prophetic preaching begins and ends with love. Love is the biggest factor in what we say and in how we say it. Paul talks about how he cared for the people—that he came to them like a gentle mother with her children. I read that and ask myself, *Do I have the gentleness, love, cherishing, and caring of a mother?* My attitude should be that these people are like my children. I don't want to offend them unnecessarily. Yet at the same time, as a good parent I may have to confront them with difficult things.

That doesn't mean that prophetic preaching always leads to positive results. In the Old Testament, prophets like Jeremiah experienced deep rejection. That pattern of rejection doesn't seem to change much in the New Testament. For instance, in Luke 6:26 Jesus says, "Woe to you when all men speak well of you, for that is how their fathers treated the false prophets." The false prophets were loved by everyone, and everyone spoke well of them. In verses 22–23 Jesus says that when they reject you, your reward is great, for that's what they did to the real prophets. So he's saying that the way people respond to us today should be similar to the way they responded to the prophets of old. There's going to be rejection. In many ways it's good to get the same response: It helps you understand that you're in a good lineage. Jesus showed that things haven't changed that much.

We serve the same God and give the same message of good news and hope, but many people will take it as bad news and reject it.

When all is said and done, as long as I'm confident my preaching was Spirit led and motivated by love for others, I can walk away and feel good about the message. I find joy and peace when I preach a hard message in love that I believe is of the Lord, even though I know it's going to be offensive to some people. In the flesh there are times when I get sad, because I know I'll lose some friends over it, but in the Spirit there's joy and confidence. If I don't face some rejection, I get more concerned.

Francis Chan is an internationally known speaker and the author of *Crazy Love* and *Forgotten God*. He is also the founder of Eternity Bible College in Simi Valley, California.

PREACHING IN THE CITY OF MAN

Mark Buchanan

Like Francis Chan, Mark Buchanan isn't afraid to tackle tough issues. In this interview Buchanan urges us to preach biblical truth without flinching. As an example of prophetic preaching, he points to the prophet Daniel, who unapologetically addressed the cultural leaders of his day—even at the risk of his own life. In the same way, we must address the hot issues of our day without diluting biblical truth.

Like Chan, Buchanan also urges us to engage our culture with love. If we don't "get the tone right," we won't lead anyone to Christ. Instead, we'll act like Jonah—the cranky prophet who merely spewed his fury on people. According to Buchanan, angry prophets "don't break hearts," but real prophets are always in "the heart-breaking business."

According to Buchanan, we'll never break and win hearts with narrow, prudish, moralistic messages. Biblical preaching always invites people into Jesus' grand "kingdom adventure." In other words, if we ask people to release their idols, we had better hand them something more adventurous and satisfying. Prophetic preachers dare to proclaim that ultimately there's nothing more heroic, attractive, and adventurous than trusting Christ.

You've written extensively about how Christians can respond to a corrupted culture. Could you summarize the two faulty responses you've identified?

Sure, Jonah and Esther serve as the two primary bad examples for engaging our culture. Jonah exhibits the approach of many conservative churches—a denunciatory and adversarial approach. You just reject the culture and then separate yourself from it. If you're somehow hauled into having an engagement [with the culture], you display Jonah's spirit of condemnation: Forty more days and God's going to get you.

Second, there's the Esther approach, and our theologically liberal brothers and sisters may have been tempted toward this. Prior to Esther's realizing that she's been raised up for such a time as this, she's really just a beauty queen. She wants to be like everyone else in the culture, only a little more so.

She hides her identity. She's embarrassed by the distinctive Jewishness of her uncle Mordecai: She sends him clothes when he's out there mourning and fasting so that he brings no reproach on her. And there has been a tendency in the church to conform, to fit in with the culture so we are never reproached by it. We stay with it; we keep up with the trends.

What are some of the warning signs of a Jonah mind-set?

Touching on an issue that's current and controversial—same-sex marriage—there's a temptation to want nothing to do with any of that. If they come near here, we'll denounce them.

If we're going to ask anybody to give up their idols, we'd better present a relationship with God and a relationship with the people of God that is worth the trade-off for them. When they feel the love they are seeking is selling them short, they may see there's a love available in Christ Jesus that is real and incarnated among the people of God.

If we take the Jonah approach, we can miss the spiritual hunger that is underneath things in our culture that are deplorable on the surface. In Acts 17 Paul goes to Athens and sees all the idols and is deeply distressed. The word for *distressed* is a very strong word in the Greek. It basically means he's having a seizure over it. And yet when he gets up to preach that night at Mars Hill, he doesn't come across as this condemnatory preacher saying, "I see how deluded and given over to corruption you are." He becomes very winsome: "I see that you're very religious, and that you even have shrines to the unknown god. I want to tell you about the God you're seeking."

There's all this questing that's very idolatrous within our culture. The Jonah approach looks only at the surface of it instead of probing to ask, how is this potentially a quest for God?

Take the Jonah story. The Ninevites are wicked people, but they are quick to repent, because underneath all of that wickedness was a false quest for the true God.

Do you feel that preachers have a responsibility to address sensitive issues—like same-sex marriage or homosexuality—from the pulpit?

Absolutely. The approach we take in our church is, if we're not taking on those issues and doing so in a way that's biblically substantive, grace-filled, Christ-centered, and giving hope without giving excuse to people, then we're participating in the ongoing irrelevance of the church to the broken world.

Jesus is clear that he's called us to be in the world not of it, and that he's sent us among highways and byways to proclaim good news to people for whom the church often doesn't come across as good news.

It is incarnational. It is seeking as Jesus himself sought: to seek and save that which is lost and to bring healing to the sick. There are ways we can engage culture that may make us feel good because we vent our spleen. But they will not advance the redemption and hope of Jesus Christ. There are ways we can do it that are highly engaging, that don't back down from the controversial aspects of the issue but don't merely inflame those things. We should bring more light than heat to the issues.

Could you share an example of this Jonah approach to engaging culture?

A couple of weeks ago, someone came to me and said, "Did you know there are two gay men attending our church?" I said, "I didn't, but that's good to hear."

And I never flinch on this issue. I'm not fuzzy on this. But it's important to me that there's a tone in which I communicate that at least piques the curiosity of people who may disagree with me. And I hope that, more than it piques their curiosity, it articulates the gospel and the hope of Christ in such a way that they say: "I may have some fundamental or visceral or philosophical or personal reasons for disagreeing with Mark Buchanan, but I believe that man loves Jesus, and I believe he loves me."

A lot of that has to do with tone. Jonah gets a one-liner from God: Forty more days and then Nineveh will die. But the tone with which he delivered that message—though it does bring repentance to the town—is anger and rancor and bitterness and resentment, and all those other things that harden hearts. They don't break hearts. And we need to be in the heart-breaking business.

In contrast, you discuss the "Esther" preachers who merely accommodate to our corrupted culture. What are some of the warning signs of preaching with this Esther mind-set?

We get shy about speaking on these issues, and we're too quick to concede ground that has always been ours to defend. Paul is clear that he is going to defend the gospel. When we feel embarrassment over the things we have to be absolutely clear and unflinching about, we're venturing toward an Esther mind-set.

And that pertains not only to doctrinal areas, but also to ethical areas where we're willing to fudge on what the Scriptures are unambiguous about. And we do that in the name of inclusiveness, et cetera, et cetera.

Lately I've been walking my church through the concept of heaven. And heaven has a radical exclusivity: Revelation 21:8 talks about who won't be there—like cowards and the sexually immoral.

But it also has a radical inclusiveness. Who will be there? The glory of the nations. And the church needs to understand that if we need to hold to that radical exclusivity, we have to call people to righteousness. We have to call people to purity. We cannot in any way dilute that.

At the same time, in some of the ways we call people to this, we're trafficking in moralism more than in purity. We're saying, "You've got to look like this: You've got to button up and sit still in your chair"—and other things that are a violation of the radical inclusiveness of heaven, where every tribe, tongue, and nation brings the splendor of who they are before the throne of God.

You've also argued that the church shouldn't attempt to impose morality but to preach purity. What does it look like for a preacher to preach purity?

For one thing, the very concept of purity is much more attractive than morality. Morality, whether this is a misunderstanding or not, seems to traffic in rules—to say, "Here are the strictures; you need to mind your p's and q's and behave yourself."

Purity calls us to a life of God-ward-ness and adventure; there's something heroic about it. There's something winsome about the life of purity.

It also has a certain currency within the culture. Bottled water companies are competing over who's got the purest product. We buy organic vegetables because we want things that are grown with the least amount of additives and preservatives. We want pure things. So, in the mind-set of the people on the street, purity is a good thing.

And if you look at what God has to say about being pure, a call to purity is much more strongly enforced than the whole thing of being moral. It's a broader concept all together. How a preacher approaches this, in the area of sexual ethics, for instance, should be as a life of purity—a life of Christ's life flowing through us. There's a vigor and robustness about it.

When I was preaching on Esther a little while ago, I was talking about how conforming to the culture will kill us in the end. I said, "I want to speak to the young women here about the way some of you dress. This is not condemnatory, but I need to ask you to help me—a red-blooded male who is attracted to your body in all the wrong ways—help me and my brothers to live a life of purity. Scripture is very clear that, if we're not sexually moral, we're actually defiling you as a sister in Christ. And we can defile you by our thoughts, and I don't want to do that, and I know my brothers don't want to do that. We're not blaming you; we're just asking you to help us. We're weak."

I got a standing ovation. And I think it was because there is a hunger for someone to speak clearly and forthrightly about it. Also, it was done in a way that nobody was shamed. They were not imposed on by a narrow morality: you trampish girls, coming in with your belly showing.

Instead, they were invited into a kingdom adventure: Can we do this together as a community? Can you understand how we, as men, are wired and serve us in the spirit of Christ? Will you do that, for Christ's sake and for our sake? Something in most people's hearts leaps toward that invitation.

Virtue rightly understood is not a narrow, confining, priggish thing. We are honoring our own body and who we are as sacred people made in the image of God. We're honoring our God, and we're honoring others.

In contrast to the Esther and Jonah mind-sets, how does Daniel display a more balanced perspective in preaching prophetically to our culture?

The Daniel story is beautiful, because Daniel is even more immersed and caught up in the pagan culture than Jonah or Esther. Jonah is still in his little enclave and gets called out of it. In Esther's story, there is still some separateness—the Jewish community is distinct from the surrounding culture.

You don't get that in Daniel's story at all. The best and the brightest are recruited, then systematically groomed and educated to fit within the pagan world—even renamed. There is entire immersion into culture. And what's fascinating about that is that Daniel can comply with some aspects and say, "That's fine; I'll go along with that," and in other areas he takes a stand. He says, "There's a point I cannot cross over; I cannot partake in that without a violation of my conscience and the God I love and worship."

And the way he does that is so winsome. It's not crusading. It's not with mouth frothing. He's quiet, he's modest, and he's hard as steel. He's adamant.

I love this picture of what the church, the people of God, can be within a fallen culture. In a lot of ways, we are recruited into perpetuating a system that we may be victims of. How can we make a stand within that system that's unambiguous without being obnoxious? Daniel gives us a brilliant portrait of what that looks like.

Does Daniel provide any lessons for how preachers can prepare their sermons?

Daniel's modesty, civility, and firmness of conviction are virtues for preachers and also those to whom they preach. As an example: Not long ago, a young man I know told me that he worked in a place that sold books of pornography. He asked me what I thought.

I said, "Let's unpack that. First of all, you have to make an abstinence commitment: I'm not going to take that to the bathroom on my break. Second, you can go to the boss, as Daniel went to the boss, and say, 'Is there any way I can get an exemption here?'" And that's what this young man did. And the non-Christian boss came under conviction and removed the stuff from his store.

We don't always have happy endings like that, but we can always go in a spirit that says: This is where I stand; these are why I hold these convictions; this is why I, in good conscience, cannot partake of such and such. Is there any way we can come to an understanding here? And if we do that with a Daniel spirit, a spirit of firmness but civility, most people are willing to meet us more than halfway.

When preaching it, there are ways we can embody that spirit in the discussion of these more controversial issues. It's all in the tone with which we speak truth. Truth can become falsehood if we don't get the tone right.

You mentioned you got a standing ovation for preaching on purity to women. Based on your experience and what you've heard from others, what happens when preachers adopt a Daniel mind-set when they focus on purity?

Our church has tons of young people. We're a very cross-generational church, and we continue to attract some of the most good-looking, well-built young people. They are finding Christ and living this Daniel life of purity.

I'm seeing that purity is attractive to people. It's hard and it requires discipline, and it takes a group of people who will walk with you, exhort you in it, and call you to account. There's nothing easy about it. But our hearts love virtue and rise to it. And I'm seeing a community forming of young men and women who are stepping up to be each other's soul mates and role models in that life.

The other thing I'm seeing is a restored sense of loveliness. The standard of the age for female and male beauty is the porno star. God's standard of beauty is loveliness, which is an inner quality. Certainly there are things you want to be aware of in terms of your dress and how you conduct yourself. But loveliness is a quality of the heart and spirit.

My heart is increasingly realizing how God has called the church to be the presence of Christ in this broken, hostile, needy world.

As a church, our mandate these days is to win the heart of our community. And the concept of winning the heart of the community is the essence of what I'm about as a preacher—to win them in Christ's power, to win a life out of darkness and destruction, to be winsome, and to portray God without censoring the revelation of God. We need to embody the message of God among our people in a way that breaks and wins hearts.

Mark Buchanan is pastor of New Life Community Baptist Church in Duncan, British Columbia, and author of numerous books, including *Spiritual Rhythm*, *The Rest of God*, *The Holy Wild*, and *Your God Is Too Safe*.

PREACHING LIKE JESUS

James MacDonald

By the time James MacDonald gets done preaching (or talking about preaching), you'll never have to ask him, "So, James, tell me, what do you really think?" MacDonald's approach to preaching is refreshingly direct, bold, and honest. It's tempting to say that MacDonald is an "authoritative preacher," but he would quickly reject that label. Instead, he'd claim, "I preach the authority of God's Word without apology."

In one way or another, you'll hear MacDonald emphasize the same theme: the authority for prophetic preaching doesn't reside in the preacher. It's not in the preacher's personality (although God can use many different personality types) or in the preacher's attempt to be relevant. The preacher's authority has one basis: the authority of God's Word. MacDonald tells us to treat God's Word like a lion: let it out of the cage, get out of the way, and it will take care of itself.

MacDonald claims that people are hungering to hear someone preach the truth of God's Word without reservation. Of course it helps that MacDonald also possesses a big heart. He says that at heart he's a "brokenhearted man preaching to brokenhearted people." The preacher's most important quality is the size of his confidence in God's Word. For MacDonald, that catalyzes the power of every prophetic sermon.

At Harvest Bible Chapel we're well aware that many people would say we live in an antiauthority culture and that people don't respond to bold preaching of God's Word. But from the very beginning of our church, we established a foundation for preaching the authority of God's Word without apology. That's very different from the phrase *preaching with authority.* I would never refer to myself as preaching with an authoritative style. But I know why people might put it that way—that comes from the unapologetic proclamation of the Word. The prophets came from the same mind-set when they constantly said, "Thus saith the LORD."

I try not to spend any time in my message preparation thinking about what people want to hear or what questions the culture is asking. I just don't have time to dwell on those questions. For more than twenty years, I've believed that if you try with all of your heart to say some things that God wants said (and of course God has some things to say; that's why he wrote a Book) God would get the people there to hear the message. Now, with some thirteen thousand people in weekly attendance, that's happening. It's been a steady journey. We never experienced explosive growth. But we also didn't have a bunch of transfer growth from other churches. Primarily Harvest Bible Chapel has watched many people come to know Christ for the first time.

Christ also preached the Word without apology. When he finished teaching, people often said that he taught as one with authority. Of course his teachings were filled with Old Testament quotes, and he is the Word of God, so naturally every word that proceeds from his mouth literally becomes the Word of

God. That's certainly not true about any of us, least of all me. After the disciples walked with Jesus on the road to Emmaus, they said, "Did not our hearts burn within us while he talked to us on the road, while he opened to us the Scriptures?" (Luke 24:32). So Jesus was a Bible preacher. He had great authority because he didn't apologize for God's Word. He didn't back down from anything that God's Word said.

I preached just two weeks ago on Revelation 6. The message had one point: Repent; the wrath is coming. That's not very seeker friendly, but I believe that people are hungry for truth, truth that is expressed without reservation or prevarication, just open and straightforward truth. Paul said, "By the open statement of the truth we would commend ourselves to everyone's conscience in the sight of God" (2 Cor. 4:2) and that's what I believe. Paul said, "My speech and my message were not in plausible words of wisdom, but in demonstration of the Spirit and of power, that your faith might not rest in the wisdom of men but in the power of God" (1 Cor. 2:4–5). A lot of preaching today leaves people with faith in the wisdom of men: Wasn't that a clever talk? Wasn't he an eloquent speaker? It glorifies the messenger. Instead, when we try to say what God wants said and get out of the way, that glorifies the message and the source of the message, which is, of course, God himself.

The delivery of a prophetic sermon

In the familiar definition, preaching is truth communicated through personality. Our personalities are different. If I sounded like you in preaching, that wouldn't be authentic; and if you sounded like me, that wouldn't be authentic. We need to be authentic to our own personalities. We don't want to come across authoritative. Whether you're meek and mild by nature or you're boisterous and strong by nature, all of those human traits need to be brought under the control of the Holy Spirit, under the conviction that gripped the apostles in the early chapters of Acts, when they said, "for we cannot but speak of what we have seen and heard" (see 4:20).

Believing that you have a life-and-death word from God brings urgency through any human vessel, regardless of personality. It brings a word of urgency that has an element of authority in it for sure, whether it's soft spoken or loud. The message may sound different coming through different people, but the authority needs to be there. I don't believe for a moment that Amos was the same as Isaiah. They're different people, and God uses all different kinds of people. The authority is in the Word of God, not in the human instrument.

The two elements of authority in preaching

But despite our personality differences, I believe that there are two elements that every preacher should have: urgency and clarity. First Corinthians says, "And if the bugle gives an indistinct sound, who will get ready for battle?" (see 14:8). Clarity brings power and the authority of God's Word. Urgency—or the sense that this message matters, so decide today—also brings the authority of God's Word.

The opposite of clarity sounds like this: "Well, um, some scholars say this, and then again some scholars say that." I don't preach interpretive options. I know there are interpretive options, and in our preparation we need to be scholarly in our consideration of those options. But preachers should come to what they believe the text means, and then they should preach that.

Walking through "some people believe this, some people believe that"—often those are such ancillary points anyway, while the main point of the text is clear and unequivocal. Spending a lot of time in these tributaries of uncertainty tends to undermine the goal of preaching, which is confidence in the Word of God.

Many people confuse the end game of preaching. The end game of preaching is not to keep people's interest. That's where a lot of people go off track. You can do all kinds of things to keep people's interest, but you're not faithfully representing the God of the Bible. So I try to keep people's interest, but that's not the end game.

Some people think the end game is relevancy. We don't make the Bible relevant; the Bible is universally relevant. We show its relevancy. The Bible is applicable to people no matter what they're facing, because God's Spirit uses it.

The end game of preaching is not being interesting or being relevant. The end game of preaching is the person's view of Scripture. The Bible is spiritual life to a person. It's nourishment; it's faith; it's victory over sin; and it's grace and strength. The Bible is our spiritual food. People are starving while preachers try to make it relevant, or they try to make it interesting. At the end of the day, I want people to see that the message of the Bible is God's Word to them, powerful and life changing. If I can lead people into the life-changing power of God's Word, they'll want to get into the Word for themselves. So the end game of preaching is simply this: to display the wealth and richness of the gifts that God has given to us in his Word. If that happens, although they can't remember my outline or the title of my message or what we preached on for the third Sunday in February, they'll still remember what they thought about this biblical passage or book when they heard it being proclaimed from the pulpit.

So the end game of preaching is a view of Scripture. A lot of guys come into the pulpit with the wrong view of Scripture themselves, so the people can't end up with a right view of Scripture.

The centrality of Scripture

If someone has a low view of Scripture, that's going to leak through everything he does. There won't be any urgency, and there won't be any clarity when there's a low view of Scripture.

Not long ago I was driving in my car listening to a local Christian radio station. A preacher was saying that people don't accept the authority of the Bible anymore, so you can't just start a sermon with "Thus says the LORD."

So the interviewer rightly asked, "Well, where do you need to start if you can't start with the Scriptures?"

He answered, "Instead of saying, 'Thus saith the LORD,' maybe sometimes you need to start with 'Thus says *The Lord of the Rings.'*"

I never call radio stations, but I was on the phone that day. They put me through and said, "James, you're on the air." I asked that preacher, "Are you saying that God's Word is not authoritative until the listener accepts its authority?"

God's Word is supernatural. We make a big mistake if we think that God's Word can't have authority until the hearer accepts its authority. When the Bible promises about itself that it is sharper than any two-edged sword, it is claiming that it can pierce through all of us, cutting right into the depths of our hearts. It separates joints and marrow; it discerns the thoughts and intents of the heart. The Bible is like a mirror. When you proclaim it without apology, with authority, you are holding up a mirror and thrusting people through with a sword, and they're going to have an encounter with God himself.

That transcends cultural acceptance, cultural awareness, and every other "nuance" that some preachers want to worry about. What they really need to do—as someone said a long time ago and I couldn't agree more—is treat the Bible like a lion: let it out of the cage, and it will take care of itself. That's what I've been doing for twenty years, and I see God bearing fruit through setting the Bible free to do its work. I see God being faithful to himself and to his Word despite the frailty and imperfections of the human messenger.

It's not about the preacher

I've heard people say to me, "Okay, sure, James, but you have a big voice, a big personality; you're a big guy. What part does physical presence play in the authority of the preacher?"

I tell my people on a monthly basis that the messenger is nothing; the message is everything. The urgency with which I am holding up God's Word has nothing to do with the strength of my voice or the size of my frame. It has to do with the amount of confidence I have that this is God's Word and that God is going to honor that.

I grew up in a church where the pastor's authority transferred over to every conversation he had. If the pastor predicted who would win the Super Bowl with the same authority he brought to his preaching, then I'd say he's an authoritarian preacher. But I don't want to be authoritarian or authoritative. I want to be a brokenhearted man preaching to brokenhearted people. If there's any fruit to my life that remains, it will be because of my abiding confidence in the Word of God and the God of the Word.

D. Martyn Lloyd-Jones said that preaching is theology on fire. Preaching is theology coming through a man who is on fire. We have plenty of sermons; what we need is people with a word from God. I frequently will weep or become emotional when I am preaching. I can't preach about something that hasn't gripped me. I was talking to a well-known pastor recently who said when he has to go out of town he just preaches his message in an empty room. I don't know how anyone does that. To me, there's a supernatural *something* going on when a pastor stands up before his people after many hours of study and prayerful reflection and says, "Open your Bibles to this passage. I have a word for you today."

For instance, we've been going through Revelation this year, and I'm telling you, it's challenging me. God has worked in our church this year through the book of Revelation like I haven't seen maybe ever, and it's just because he's honoring his Word.

The anointing of the Holy Spirit in prophetic preaching

The Bible says that the Spirit of God was sent into the world to convict people of their sin. That's something we need to see happen more often: *conviction*. The goal of a preacher's message is that at some point people would feel convicted. Conviction implies that people are overcome with the gaps that exist between the lives they're living and the lives God wants them to live. Conviction can happen at the entry point of the gospel or at some point in the process of progressive sanctification.

Scripture says that the Spirit of God was sent into the world to convict of sin and of righteousness and of the judgment to come. Sin is the wrong in me; righteousness is its opposite in me. Sin is the problem; righteousness is the solution. The judgment to come is the consequence of rejecting what the Spirit convicts me of in regard to sin and righteousness. Sin is where I am; righteousness is where I need to be; and judgment to come is the sense that I can't leave it like that forever. That's what the Spirit is trying to produce in people.

It's the proclamation of the Word that brings that conviction, and there's nothing else that can do that. When we proclaim the authority of God's Word without apology, we give the Spirit of God something to work with. God never promised to bless *my* thoughts or *my* insights. The Spirit of God will grip my heart with the message, and then as I proclaim it—truth coming through a yielded vessel, hopefully—then he's taking and using that to bring other people to the same place that he's brought me.

So he convicts me first, and then he convicts others. But the Bible passage works me over every week before it convicts anyone else. Preaching the Word of God in one church for more than twenty years has been the crucible of my sanctification, without question. I've got 1,500 messages in a drawer there. I could go on the road anytime, but that would be the death of me spiritually.

The main point of prophetic preaching

I'm not trying to quibble over words, but I would never use the term *preaching with authority*. That ascribes authority to the messenger, and the authority is not in the messenger. The authority is in the Word. I hope if you hung out with me and we spent time together, you'd see a marked gap between the tonality of my preaching, where I'm speaking for God and representing him, and the tonality of my private conversation. It shouldn't be the same. The authority should be in the message, not in the messenger.

I never listen to another preacher and think to myself, *How could he be more authoritative?* What I sometimes do, though, is I listen to a preacher equivocate about God's Word, and I think to myself, *What an awful business it must be to have to get up and teach a message from a Book that you don't even believe, or that has portions you don't believe.* To me, if you don't believe portions of it, then what good is it at that point? It's not supernatural; it's just a human document, so let's go golfing. I wouldn't want to spend my life preaching something I don't think is a message from God.

If I ever think that another preacher sounds spiritually weak—not because he offers comfort or encouragement but because he's hesitant about what he's saying about God's Word—I also think to myself, *low view of Scripture.*

Over the past twenty years, I've known significant leaders within Christianity who knowingly or unknowingly deemphasized the centrality of the Word of God. I've also seen that when any ministry deemphasizes the priority and centrality of God's Word it won't last for long. Jesus said, "Heaven and earth will pass away, but my words will not pass away" (Luke 21:33). God himself is supernaturally preserving his Word in the center of the work that truly belongs to his kingdom.

Where the Word is deemphasized, ministries are doomed. They're doomed. They're paddling toward the falls, and they don't even know it. They're not confident in God's Word. Their ministry is not going anywhere good. There are preachers who have been loose and free and cavalier with the explicit statements of Scripture, and they've been celebrated from coast to coast, but their ministries and their lives are in a free fall—already, in our lifetime. God does not sustain such a ministry. "For the eyes of the LORD run to and fro throughout the whole earth, to give strong support to those whose heart is blameless toward him" (2 Chron. 16:9). God is not going to strongly support someone who does not strongly support his Word.

James MacDonald is founding and senior pastor of Harvest Bible Chapel in Rolling Meadows, Illinois, a radio speaker for *Walk in the Word*, and the author of numerous books, including *God Wrote a Book* and *When Life Is Hard*.

GRACE-FULL PROPHETIC PREACHING

Bryan Loritts

In 2003 Bryan Loritts moved to the heart of Memphis and planted a multiethnic, multigenerational church. It was a gutsy venture. According to Loritts, Memphis had a highly churched but shallow, moralistic view of Christianity—like a thin, shiny layer of varnish slapped on hollow wood. And to make matters worse, Memphis (Loritts calls it "Churchville, USA") was one of the most racist, segregated places in the country.

In the midst of these challenges, Loritts rediscovered the most powerful source for personal and societal transformation: preaching the gospel and the personal presence of Jesus. Prophetic preaching strips away the veneer of religion, shatters our perceptions of church, and lays bare our arrogant and racist "elder brother mind-sets." The gospel sets us free from the exhausting treadmill of religious performance. Of course that doesn't happen by using the Word of God as a "sledgehammer to bludgeon people." For Loritts, prophetic preachers confront sin and call people to repent, but they also come as instruments of God's grace. When we preach the centrality of the cross, it challenges all

of us—black and white, young and old, rich and poor—to repent,
trust Christ, live by grace, and then build God's counter-cultural
and multiethnic community.

Prophetic preaching in "Churchville, USA"

Prophetic preaching is a great term, but you have to explain it, because the term *prophetic* has several connotations. Do you mean prophetic in the sense of foretelling or in the sense of forth telling? Prophetic preaching is forth telling. Whether you see yourself as a prophetic preacher or not, anyone who stands and opens up the Bible and says, "Here's what God says," is really taking on the mantle of a prophet. In the Old Testament when the prophets came, they always came saying, "Here's what God is saying."

Let me explain what I mean by talking about prophetic preaching in my context. I pastor a church in Memphis. They say the average city has one church per thousand people; Memphis has two. I call Memphis "Churchville, USA," because it's a highly religious place. Yet as churched as it is, Memphis is one of the most racist, segregated places in the country. So in my sermons I have to address the following questions: What has religion, what has church, done the wrong way? What has it accomplished for the city? Based on the evidence, you'd have to conclude that the church isn't that different from the surrounding culture.

So one thing we're preaching on this year is the gospel. Not that we didn't preach the gospel before, but we wanted to take a twelve-month run at confronting cultural Christianity, moralism, religion—the "elder brother" mind-set that is rampant in Memphis—and juxtapose that with the gospel. So this whole year has been somewhat confrontational, because people are having their perceptions of what church and Christianity is all about completely shattered by the reality of the gospel. Specifically we're running through the Sermon on the Mount and juxtaposing religion with what Jesus teaches about the gospel.

Prophetic preaching in the Old Testament

Of course I'm not doing anything brand new; there's plenty of prophetic preaching from the Old Testament prophets. They had incredible courage and boldness to stand in front of people and say, "I'm going to tell you something you probably won't like, but I'm on assignment and I've got to do it anyways." You couldn't be a people pleaser and do what the prophets did. That gives me comfort, knowing that I'm standing on assignment from God. I can't lead people and be scared of them at the same time. I've got to speak the truth of God, because I love them dearly.

The prophets get a bad rap, because when you think *prophetic*, you think *black and white*; you think of something that is only condemning or critical. But Old Testament prophecy is really an incredible picture of grace. The prophet's punch line was always something like this: "Here's what God is going to do, so get your act together and avoid it." So the prophet came not primarily to condemn people. Yes, he called out sin, but he came as an instrument of God's grace. Prophetic preaching says: The very fact that you're still alive today is God's way of saying there's time for you to turn around.

In my context, I resonate with the prophet Jonah. Sometimes God assigns you to minister to people that in your flesh you would not enjoy being around. When Jonah went to Nineveh, he did not like the Ninevites. They were the oppressors. He wanted to open his mouth, spew forth the Word of the Lord, step back, and watch God zap them. That's why he gets upset when God shows kindness to people who were oppressing the Jews.

Honestly, as an African-American preaching in a multicultural context, my passion comes out of my wounds. I've experienced some hurtful things in the past from my white brothers and sisters, but God is in the process of healing those wounds. Historically there are some similarities between whites in this country and the Assyrians, in that whites were in the position of power and they abused that power. Yet God, as he did with Jonah, is sending me, a minority, to preach prophetically and yet graciously the cross of Jesus Christ to a group of people who used to oppress us. That encourages me when I'm tempted to bitterness like Jonah succumbed to.

The dangers of prophetic preaching

But that doesn't mean that prophetic preaching can't get off track. Jesus has three offices: prophet, priest, and king. Jesus definitely wore the mantle of a prophet, yet John says that Jesus was also a man full of grace and truth. Prophetic preaching gets off track when I use the Word of God as a sledgehammer to bludgeon people, when there's no graciousness in how I present the truth.

Some pastors who see themselves as prophetic preachers only see the world in terms of right and wrong. There's a temptation to get into legalism, to be regimented, to see issues only in black and white categories—especially things that the Bible doesn't speak clearly about and that aren't essential matters of faith. At our church we talk about essentials versus nonessentials. We say in a loving way that we're not budging on the essentials, but when it comes to nonessentials, we have to say, "As we study the Scriptures, we don't see God speaking clearly on that."

When the prophet spoke to the people, there was only one thing he could hold onto: "I know what God said to me. That's what I've got to preach. I've got to preach with clarity what God is clear on. On anything else I may present my opinion, but I can't be as black and white." Prophetic preaching derails when it starts speaking forcefully about stuff that the Scriptures don't address forcefully.

Mentored in the art of prophetic preaching

I learned about the nature and pitfalls of prophetic preaching through some specific people who mentored my preaching. Three men have had the biggest influence in my life. Of course my dad [Crawford Loritts, pastor of Fellowship Bible Church in Roswell, Georgia] had the biggest influence on my life as a preacher. I grew up the son of not just a preacher but a great preacher, and not just a great preacher but a great person. My dad would be the first to call out truth, but he'd be the first to take his shirt off his back and help the less fortunate. I've seen my dad weep in the pulpit.

When I said I wanted to be a pastor, my dad said to me, "Son, I'm not a pastor (at the time he wasn't, now he is), but I've got a pastor friend who can help you." It was Kenneth Ulmer [pastor of Faithful Central Bible Church in Inglewood, California], and I sat under him. He influenced me powerfully, and he has a strong prophetic ministry.

Tony Evans [pastor of Oak Cliff Bible Fellowship in Dallas, Texas], a friend of our family, also shaped my thinking and practice of preaching prophetically. I spent a summer working with him.

I've also had people who shaped my preaching through their books and writings. Henri Nouwen and Timothy Keller are authors who have had a huge impact in helping me understand the gospel. Again, the gospel is prophetic, because it deals with sin and calls people to repentance, which is what the prophets did.

A. W. Tozer has been incredibly helpful as well. I've also read biographies on great preachers who functioned in a prophetic way, like Spurgeon. I read Lewis Drummond's *Spurgeon: Prince of Preachers*. The two-volume work *George Whitefield: The Life and Times of the Great Evangelist of the Eighteenth-Century Revival*, written by Arnold Dallimore and published by Banner of Truth, was extremely helpful. Banner of Truth also published a two-volume biography of D. Martyn Lloyd-Jones, written by Iain H. Murray. I devoured those books.

I love what Charles Spurgeon said when asked, in today's terminology, about his "operating system" for preaching. He said, "I take my text and make a beeline for the cross." I want to lift up the glory and splendor of the cross. I want to get people to see that in Christ they are accepted, they are God's beloved, and that they have all that they need. They need to get off the moralism track.

G. K. Chesterton said, "Jesus Christ did not die to make bad people good; he died to make dead people alive." In Memphis that really resonates with people, because there's this sense that if I go to the right church, if I go to that Bible study, if I get the radio preacher bobble heads, then I will be a good enough person. The gospel shatters all that, and it does it in a way that people are relieved. They can finally get off the treadmill of religion.

Bryan Loritts is the Lead Pastor for Fellowship Memphis, the author of *God on Paper*, and a contributing author of *Great Preaching*.

PREACHING LIKE A PROPHET

John Ortberg

It's tough to deny that the Old Testament prophets often acted weird. Hosea married a prostitute. Isaiah walked around naked. Jeremiah couldn't stop crying. Amos called the leading rich folks a bunch of "fat cows." The Old Testament prophets also kept dredging up touchy topics like idolatry, sexual immorality, and injustice toward the poor. No wonder people wanted to kill them or just ignore them.

Apparently things haven't changed much. Why do we still feel uncomfortable around contemporary prophets? In this chapter John Ortberg contends that most of us see the world's deep pain—children with HIV, sprawling inner-city slums, corrupt business practices—and we merely shrug our shoulders. But compelled by Christ's love, prophetic preachers see the "crushing burden" of injustice, and it breaks their hearts. Ortberg wants us to pause and reflect: Do we see the world's brokenness? Do we look through Jesus' eyes? Or have we already turned away?

But Ortberg doesn't just want us to feel compassion for the world's pain; he also wants us to remain connected to the living God, the Source of prophetic passion. Otherwise our prophetic preaching will mimic the tired and contentious political agendas of our culture.

Who needs the church to do that? Instead, when we're grounded in the gospel, especially the cross and resurrection of Jesus, we can offer the world something radically fresh and eternally good.

Think about the basic human emotions we get to preach on: joy, sadness, comfort, anger, and serenity. Now think about the prophets—which emotion most often characterizes them? Consider a few examples:

> "Hear this word, you cows of Bashan on Mount Samaria,
>   you women who oppress the poor and crush the needy
>   and say to your husbands, 'Bring us some drinks!'"
>   (Amos 4:1)

> "Stop bringing meaningless offerings!
>   Your incense is detestable to me.
> . . . I cannot bear your evil assemblies."
>   (Isa. 1:13)

> "Should you not know justice,
>   you who hate good and love evil;
> who tear the skin from my people
>   and the flesh from their bones;
> who eat my people's flesh,
>   strip off their skin,
>   and break their bones in pieces;
> who chop them up like meat for the pan?"
>   (Mic. 3:1–3)

Don't the prophets strike you as kind of cranky? Not only do they use angry words, prophets resort to shock tactics that often look downright bizarre:

- Hosea marries a prostitute to show how unfaithful the people have become.

- Ezekiel eats food cooked over excrement to show people how defiled they've become.

- Jeremiah digs up a filthy, buried, unwashed undergarment to show people how repulsive their behavior was.

The prophets are filled with this stuff. No wonder those of us who preach often avoid them. Our listeners don't always like it. We don't like it. (Does anyone really want to encourage such prophet-like behavior in one's congregation?)

We like happy books. In most of our churches, it is easier to preach comfort than judgment, mercy than justice, because by the standards of God's justice, who can ever measure up?

On the other hand, these passages are in the Bible. In fact the prophets directly account for 250 of the 1,189 chapters in the Bible. Can you really be a biblical preacher and not address what the prophets have to say?

Why we must preach on justice

More than that, there is a reason why we need to preach on justice. There is a reason for the anger of the prophets, and why we need to submit ourselves to the discipline of regularly sitting under and preaching their words.

Imagine you're listening to someone sing. They are singing off-key, badly off-key, and they're singing loudly. If you are musically insensitive—have a tin ear—it doesn't bother you much. If you are musically insensitive and the singer is your grandchild, it may actually make you very pleased.

But if you have perfect pitch—it's a different story. You know what the song could be, should be. You know how far it's off. You look at tin-eared grandma and wonder, *How can she stand to listen to this?*

This is painful. You're in agony.

We read the prophets and think: *What's the big deal? What are they getting all heated up about?*

To us the world is not so bad. Most of us are pretty happy. Things are going okay—at least for me. I know there's violence in the world. It's regrettable, but as long as it doesn't touch my life, I would prefer not to think much about it. Certainly that's not connected to my anger, self-centeredness, lack of love.

Cheating goes on every day in business. Somebody shades the truth a little for profit; that's just the way things are. Some eight thousand children are born with or infected with HIV every day in sub-Saharan Africa, and it's now the leading cause of death. A few miles away from my church, from any church, children are born in poverty, living in ghettos or slums; they will grow up without access to decent education and housing. But they're not my children. Maybe their parents did something to deserve it. So what if in ancient Israel the poor often got the shaft? Where is it any different? Why go off the deep end?

The prophets act like the world is falling apart. What's the big deal?

The prophets have been given the crushing burden of looking at our world and seeing what God sees: rich people trying to get richer and looking the other way while poor people die. And thinking God is really pretty pleased with their lives, that the world is going pretty well.

We tend to avoid preaching about justice, because we don't really want to know the truth about what sin has done to our world and to us. Because that would make us uncomfortable. As Micah 2:11 puts it:

> If a liar and deceiver comes and says,
>   "I will prophesy for you plenty of wine and beer,"
>   he would be just the prophet for this people!

We prefer preaching that tastes great and is less filling. To paraphrase the great scholar Abraham Heschel, "The shallowness of our moral comprehension, the incapacity to sense the depth of misery caused by our own failures, is a simple fact of fallen humanity which no explanation can cover up."

Events that horrified the prophets go on every day in our world, but we just get used to it—like you get used to wearing your watch. After a while—we don't notice anymore.

The prophets noticed. The prophets never got desensitized to sin. Injustice is sin. Justice is central to shalom. We omit justice from our preaching at peril of our calling, and of our congregation's health and ability to see the reality around them.

Why preaching about justice is hard

But . . . there are a host of challenges in preaching about justice. Our society has become so politicized that people often hear words like *justice* or *life* or *the poor* or *compassion* as code words for a partisan political allegiance in one direction or another. Preaching about justice can drift quickly into self-righteous moralism. Many people claim the spiritual gift of prophecy when what they really have are anger management issues. There is a thin line sometimes between being a prophet and being a jerk.

Generational issues can come into play. Older members of a congregation may have been part of a denomination that drifted away from orthodox belief and replaced it with a social agenda. They may have been shaped by this experience, much as children of the Depression are forever marked in their financial lives. So talk about "justice" may bring alarm to some members, where absence of such talk may produce alarm in others.

Preaching about justice can also play into a dangerous trend in our day where ideological correctness replaces character development. People may mistake being on the "right side" of social issues with having a transformed mind and heart.

Concern for justice must also be rooted in Jesus and tied to Scripture. Historian Mark Noll noted that one shortcoming of the abolition movement was a failure to do the exegetical and theological work needed to base abolitionism in the authority of Scripture. As a result, reform movements after the Civil War (from women's rights to temperance to child labor) became increasingly detached from Scripture, and they became increasingly separated from the concerns of the church.

So how do we preach about justice in ways that can unite and inspire and form Christ more deeply in our congregations?

Justice is not partisan politics

Sociologist James Davison Hunter has written a tour-de-force critique of evangelicalism and culture called *To Change the World*. He argues that in our society the public square has become so politicized that people assume all public expressions of art or literature or religion can be placed on a political spectrum from left to right. This means that—unless we preach with great skill—our listeners will assume that words like *justice* or *poverty* or *sexuality* or *life* or *righteous* are really code words for a partisan political position.

We will have to explain that the values embedded in the Bible do not necessarily have a straight-line translation into legislation. For instance, all followers of Jesus are obligated to be concerned for the poor. But that does not mean that they should all be committed to passing a higher minimum-wage law. Very bright economists disagree about whether such legislation actually results in helping the poor. As preachers, we do not further the cause of the authority of Scripture when we pretend to be experts over fields we have not mastered.

For more than twenty-five years, Walt Gerber was the senior pastor of the church where I now serve. He had a wonderful phrase in this regard: "This is a Jesus church." Anytime someone wanted to push for a political agenda, Walt would remind the congregation that we desire to be a place where anybody—regardless of political affiliation—could come to learn about God. "This is a Jesus church."

A call to action is not asking a favor

Our church recently did a six-week series on justice issues (poverty, pandemics, care for creation, etc.). I started one of the messages by noting a Nicholas Kristof *New York Times* column in which he describes two people. Richard, a handsome and single thirty-six-year-old, works as a commodities trader and lives in Hawaii. In the midst of his busy work schedule, he finds time to date gorgeous women and spend Christmas vacation in Tahiti. In stark contrast, Lorna, a sixty-four-year-old overweight black woman, lives in Minot, North Dakota. Although Lorna is on regular dialysis, this happily married woman gives generously of her time and money to serve her grandchildren, her local church, and even global missions.

The first question was, which of these two would our society put forward as an example of the good life—which one would companies want to use as a spokesperson to say, "If you buy our product you can have their life"—Richard or Lorna?

The next question was, which one is more likely to be happy? Here's where the research gets interesting. Gender has no impact on happiness. Climate and weather have no impact on happiness. (Yes, it's cold in North Dakota, but people are actually happy there.) Beautiful people are not happier than ugly people. Younger people are actually a bit less happy than older people.

Instead, it turns out that happiness is tied to volunteering, to donating, to giving blood, to serving others. People with vital faith in God tend to be more joyful than those without.

For example, Dr. Stephen Post heads an institute that has funded high-level research on human compassion at more than forty-four major universities. The remarkable bottom line of the science of love is that *giving* protects overall health twice as much as aspirin protects against heart disease. He says the benefits of compassion just to your physical health alone are so strong that if compassion weren't free, pharmaceutical companies would herald the discovery of a stupendous new drug called "Give Back" instead of Prozac.

So to return to Nicholas Kristof's article, Lorna will most likely live longer, be happier, have more friends, experience more purpose, nurse fewer regrets. But that's not what matters most.

When we ask people to involve themselves in justice issues, we are not adding a burden on to their busy lives or asking them to do the church a favor. Ultimately what matters most is a third question: Which person is more like God—Richard or Lorna?

God himself has a certain kind of character. In that same sermon series on the Bible and justice, we simply ended up walking through the character of God, and I asked people to give God a 1 to 10 rating on:

- Compassion

- Commitment to justice

- Concern for the poor

- Generosity

- Love

By the time we had looked through Scripture on these issues, all of us were ready to say "uncle." So our concern for justice must start with and flow out of the character of God rather than any fashionable but merely human agenda.

Make justice concrete

In some churches, where many attendees are well off, we may have to remind ourselves of how badly injustice stings. Sometimes it happens in mundane and funny ways. There's a true story about a guy named Dave Hagler who served as an umpire in a softball league in Boulder, Colorado. One winter he was driving too fast in the snow, and a policeman issued him a ticket. He tried to talk the officer out of it, but the officer told him that if he didn't like it, he could go to court.

The first game of the season that Hagler umpired, the first batter to come to the plate was the police officer. They both recognized each other. The officer asked, "How did the thing with the ticket go?"

Hagler replied, "You better swing at everything."

We hate it when someone treats us unfairly—at work, in family. In contrast, the call of Jesus compels us to get as energized about someone else's being the victim of injustice as we are when it's us. In particular, Jesus calls us to be concerned about injustice for those you might be inclined to overlook—or even despise.

This is another concrete story, from a woman quoted in Miroslav Volf's wonderful book *Exclusion and Embrace*:

> I am a Muslim, and I am 35 years old. To my second son, I gave the name Jihad so he would not forget the testament of his mother—revenge. The first time I put my baby at my breast I told him, "May this milk choke you if you forget." So be it. The Serbs taught me to hate. [She describes her work as a teacher and how the very people she taught and cared for became her enemies.] My student Zoran, the only son of my neighbor, urinated into my mouth. As the bearded hooligans standing around laughed, he told me: "You are good for nothing else, you stinking Muslim woman."

That's how most of the world operates: We heap vengeance and contempt on people who have hurt us, or the people we don't like. Jesus often surprised his followers by being concerned for those whom others were inclined to overlook. On the cross we see most clearly God's hatred of injustice; and an empty tomb proclaims most loudly justice's final victory.

Provide an opportunity for action

At our church we began an experiment five years ago where we shut down our worship services one weekend a year and worshiped God by serving folks all around the San Francisco Bay area. For us, there was something about not holding services for a weekend that got people's attention, and we have close to as many people serving on Compassion Weekend as we would have attending on a normal weekend. Interestingly, an increasing percentage of those folks are from outside our church and often are searching in their own spiritual lives.

On another weekend, one of our pastors, Kevin Kim, was preaching about justice and invited people to take out their cell phones during the sermon (a practice I don't normally encourage) and text a donation to a ministry that fights sex trafficking. The only challenge was an unexpected need to do an impromptu tutorial on texting donations. But people loved being able to take immediate action.

When preaching justice, one experience can be worth a thousand sermons.

Justice points to Jesus

Maybe the most important message for me to remember in preaching is that justice matters because of Jesus. His kingdom is a place where justice prevails, so I cannot love him without loving the justice he prizes.

So we are to remind people that it is in Jesus that justice prevails. The cross was the scene of the most monstrous injustice in history, where the one truly innocent person in history was visited with the sum total of human sin.

It is on a cross we see most clearly God's hatred of injustice. It is an empty tomb that proclaims most loudly justice's final victory. And so Jesus' people are called to form a community where shalom prevails. I love the translation Eugene Peterson gives in

Acts 2 of the way the world looked on the early church and "in general liked what they saw" (Acts 2:47).

May that happen again in our day!

John Ortberg is senior pastor of Menlo Park Presbyterian Church in Menlo Park, California, a featured preacher for PreachingToday. com, and the author of *The Me I Want to Be, If You Want to Walk on Water, You've Got to Get Out of the Boat,* and *The Life You've Always Wanted.*

WHAT ALL GOOD PREACHERS DO

Craig Brian Larson

We've all heard those preachers—angry, frustrated, bombastic preachers who seem to take pride in their ability to offend people. Craig Brian Larson calls them the self-appointed moral cops. They're almost always against this and against that. Nobody wants to preach like them.

On the other hand, Larson argues that good pastors better be against something. Good doctors don't just promote health; they also fight disease. In the same way, all good pastors have at least one thing in common: they fight against the disease of doctrinal error. Like watchdogs, pastors can be loyal and affectionate, but when a burglar enters the house, they better start barking. Sadly, as the prophet Isaiah once claimed, preachers, the community's guard dogs, sometimes act like "mute dogs [that] cannot bark" (Isa. 56:10).

Based on these images, Larson wants to challenge and then dismantle a prevailing myth about preaching: that we don't need to preach against anything. It's the illusion that if we just stay positive and upbeat, our people will grow in Christ. Unfortunately that leaves our people vulnerable to attack. Prophetic preachers keep on the lookout as they ask: What are the intruders in our house? What are the diseases raging war against this body of believers?

By preaching against false doctrine, prophetic preachers protect the church. It's one way that pastors follow Jesus, the One who said, "While I was with them, I protected them and kept them safe" (John 17:12).

Recently I listened to an internet-based talk show interview with a Bible scholar. The host of the program was earnestly contending for the truth. While I liked what I heard from the Bible scholar, the host-interviewer disturbed me, not by what he said but by his manner. Not only was he melodramatic; he sounded smugly sure of himself. When I react negatively to someone who is concerned about theological discernment, I can't help but wonder how others react to my preaching, for my messages also seek not only to encourage, inform, and inspire in a positive way but also to divide truth from error.

At those times when I clearly call error error, do others perceive me as a "fundamentalist" on a crusade? As a self-appointed authority trying to police others? As insecure, angry, or arrogant?

I hope not. I want to be generous. I want to be humble.

But I also want to be good.

The reality of false teaching

For several months I have been reading and rereading 1 Timothy, and one verse that has caught my attention—and gives me pause—is Paul's words to Timothy in 4:6: "If you point these things out to the brothers, you will be a good minister of Christ Jesus, brought up in the truths of the faith and of the good teaching that you have followed."

According to this verse, to be "a good minister of Christ Jesus" I must teach certain truths and correct certain errors with the people entrusted to my care. Paul implies that if I fail to teach these things, I am not a good minister; I am—gulp—a bad minister. In this passage Paul's curriculum consists of a series of warnings (4:1–5) about the false teachings that forbid marriage and the eating of certain foods. Paul saw these ascetic teachings, which reflect an unbiblical dualism, as so harmful to believers that for pastors to fail to inoculate the flock against them was apparently a case of neglect, an oversight that disqualifies them as good ministers. It doesn't take much imagination to see why Paul required this for pastors, because not only were sound moral standards at stake in this false teaching, but also likely the nature of the gospel: Could someone be saved who ate bacon sandwiches and tied the knot with her main squeeze? The false teachers probably said no.

Today, while legalism always beckons, the legalistic demand for asceticism is not a prevailing heresy, at least not in Western culture. But that doesn't make this text irrelevant for "good ministers." The clear implication is that we must recognize the toxic teachings of our day and address them.

Paul knew precisely what false teachings threatened the Ephesian church where Timothy pastored. Can I list the ideas that threaten our church in Chicago? As I reflected on 1 Timothy 4 I realized that I had never thought through this question intentionally and determined the ideas that I and others regarded as most dangerous. Nor had I made plans to be sure I did hazmat duties on these ideas recurrently in our church. So I made a list and began a sermon series titled The Most Dangerous Ideas in Your World. Here are some of the ideas I covered in that series:

- Jesus is not God.

- If you are a good person, God will accept you.

- Everyone, or almost everyone, will be accepted by God and live in heaven forever.

- There are many paths to God, and all religions lead to him.

- We cannot know truth.

Forces that muzzle our voices

The rationale for Paul's directive to Timothy is airtight, of course. If the Centers for Disease Control (CDC) knew of a virulent flu carried by a number of people in Brooklyn but said nothing, medical heads would roll in Atlanta. If the CDC tried in vain to get media outlets to make an emergency announcement about the virus, but the media execs all refused to interrupt their entertainment because it might hurt their ratings during sweeps week, the public outcry could be heard by the deaf. For people in responsibility, failing to warn those in their care about a grave danger constitutes gross negligence that merits immediate dismissal and criminal prosecution. What's more, in the case of spiritual leaders, what is at stake is not a few more years of carbon consumption on earth but an eternity in paradise or perdition.

Still, as obvious as this is, Western culture is slogging its way through moral fog and quicksand. Our culture frowns upon calling a dangerous teaching what it is. Do that specifically from the pulpit, and some in the congregation think, *hate-speech, mean-spirited bloggers, the Salem witch hunts,* and *the Inquisition. Unity is found in centered-set categories, not bounded-set categories. Can't we all get along? Can't we be positive and constructive, agree to disagree, and hold tolerance and pluralism dear? What will this do to attendance? Aren't you being an uptight fundamentalist? Cool people don't act as though they are right and others are wrong, at least when it comes to ultimate truth. Who gives you the right to tell the world's story? There is no universal truth. Morality is relative to each society.* On and on it goes.

At the bleak shore of this swelling tide of quicksand stands the apostle Paul telling pastors to oppose certain doctrines. These doctrines are so hazardous to the true faith that pastors must warn people to avoid them just as an eighty-year-old would avoid kissing the moist lips of a feverish, red-eyed, runny-nosed, sneezing, coughing carrier of swine flu. No less diseased in our day, for instance, is the seductive idea that human beings are basically good.

Isaiah 56:10 says,

> Israel's watchmen are blind,
>   they all lack knowledge;
> they are all mute dogs,
>   they cannot bark.

According to this text, and 1 Timothy 4, even in a postmodern world, there is a time for watchmen to bark.

Some argue: If I emphasize the positive and teach the truth about the gospel, people will see heresies for what they are. I don't need to preach negatively against falsehood. That seems to make sense, but apparently Paul didn't believe it, nor did Jesus. Both explicitly warned people against dangerous ideas (see, e.g., Matt. 5–7; 23; 16:11–12; 1 Tim. 6:20; Titus 1:9–14). Both regarded false ideas as toxic (see Matt. 7:15; 2 Tim. 2:16–18). Clearly, while

CRAIG BRIAN LARSON

both Paul and Jesus taught in constructive, inspiring ways, they also engaged in the negative deconstruction of error.

And there's an enduring, culture-transcending reason for that: syncretism, the attempted fusion of what cannot fuse. Our fallen nature is such that we want to add what is true while clinging to what is false. We want right and wrong (our personal wrongs, at any rate) to be compatible. We don't realize that error compromises truth.

Principles for guarding the church

So in this confused Western culture, is there any way to be a good minister of Christ Jesus without being shunned?

For one thing, we have to engage the quicksand of ideas that says we can't call some ideas false. That's a huge topic all its own, naturally, so we can't do it at length in many sermons. But if we just ignore that assumption of many who hear us, we will be shrugged off.

In addition, our hearts must be right. We need to be walking closely with the Lord in a spirit of humility, love, and joy; these of course are minimal aspects of godliness that should characterize Christian leaders at all times, and they are especially important to disarm those who see those who refute error as arrogant, bigoted, cold, grim, and mean. This is a topic all to itself that I can't here develop further, but suffice it to say here that true Christlike maturity cuts the ground from under those who have good cause to dislike unwinsome preachers.

We must be bold and unapologetic. Faithful interpreters of Scripture are on the side of truth, and sooner or later, in his own time, God will make sure that truth wins out. The responsibility of the preacher is simply to proclaim the truth always and openly regardless of the response, to attempt to persuade if possible, and to do so in love, in humility (because it's God's truth, not ours), and, yes, with authority (seriously, firmly, strongly). Humility and confidence about the knowability of truth are not mutually exclusive.

While correcting major errors is crucial, it is not everything. In some seasons of the church, in some environments, in some sermon series or classes, this aim will necessarily prevail over all others, as was needed by Timothy in Ephesus. After all, it does little good to preach a comforting sermon from Psalm 23 to a raving heretic. But pastoral preaching that feeds the flock a balanced diet of the Word is not just a cult-watching ministry. One hesitation I have about those who take this ministry seriously is the way some can seem to be predominantly negative, very good at finding fault but handicapped at positively equipping believers to live radiant, compassionate, Spirit-empowered lives in their daily world. Pastoral preachers must positively comfort and encourage, inspire and give hope.

Finally, we must recognize the difference between (1) the central doctrines of the faith historically shared by orthodox believers, such as the deity of Jesus Christ, (2) the doctrines important or distinctive to our own wing of the orthodox church, such as the cessation or continuation of some spiritual gifts, which true believers may disagree on and thus find it difficult to organize ministry together and share regular worship, and (3) the doctrines that have traditionally been called matters of indifference, the teachings that should not break fellowship among believers of any stripe, such as beliefs about the tribulation. We address each category accordingly.

When Jesus spoke about his role in the world, one of his most important self-designations was that of shepherd for the sheep, and one of the shepherd roles he highlighted was that of offering protection. Nearing the end of his life, Jesus prayed about his disciples in John 17 and said, "While I was with them, I protected them" (17:12). That is one reason why, when Jesus called himself a shepherd, he could add the word *good*.

Craig Brian Larson is editor of PreachingToday.com and pastor of Lake Shore Church in Chicago, Illinois.

THE CLINT EASTWOODS
OF THE PULPIT?

Lee Eclov

In a poem titled "To Live in the Mercy of God," Denise Levertov compared God's mercy to a waterfall

> flinging itself unabating
> down and down. . . .
> hour after year after century.

God's "not mild, not temperate" but fierce mercy crashes on our hearts with passionate joy—even when we resist it with boulder-like stubbornness.

Lee Eclov also uses poetic metaphors to capture the wild, relentless passion of prophetic preachers. They, too, fling themselves on our stubborn hearts. Prophetic preachers barge into our lives with a life-or-death urgency about God's Word. But that doesn't mean that they merely give more and louder "you-better-shape-up-or-else" sermons. Instead, they keep pointing to the incredibly good news of Jesus. In the process, every sermon should "stir a yearning for Christ and a vision of Christ."

Eclov also urges us to remember the future dimension of prophetic preaching. Many of the chapters in this book stress that prophetic preaching focuses on today; it isn't just predictions about future events. But Eclov also argues that it isn't just about current issues; it points forward to the end of history and the hope of God's victory. Thus prophetic preaching should view the world through the dual lens of current and future events. If we fail to declare those beautiful future promises from God's Word, we'll blunt the passion and hope of the biblical prophets—including the ultimate prophet, King Jesus.

We get our mental pictures of preaching from different places in the Bible. There's Paul on Mars Hill reasoning for the faith. And there he is preaching in a synagogue laying open gospel doctrine with his finger on an Old Testament text. Over there, on the hillside, is Jesus preaching to the multitudes with crowd-quieting authority and insight ("You have heard it said . . . but I say . . ."). Follow him awhile, and we'll hear him turn a conversation toward a parable, compact and elegant. Then there is Peter on Pentecost preaching his heart out in the first full-bodied evangelistic sermon. Next thing you know, three thousand are baptized.

But there is another kind of preaching that watches Nathan with his finger in David's face ("You are the man!"); that watches Jeremiah, whose words and heart cracked flintlike against Israel's hard hearts till the sparks flew. This is preaching that takes its cues from Elijah and Isaiah and all their major and minor colleagues, right down to John the Baptist hammering away with "repent." To paraphrase the poet James Weldon Johnson, it's like "Sledgehammers of truth beating on the iron hearts of sin." This is prophetic preaching.

Nonpreachers who hear that phrase often think we mean preaching about the end times. We'll get to that, but to me prophetic preaching is pointed preaching about fundamental issues with a life-or-death urgency. But I confess it also seems to bark to the preacher, "Wipe that silly grin off your face. Ditch the cute illustration about the little girl in Sunday school, and don't even think about using that movie clip. This is serious." It is like being the cop in people's rearview mirror. I think of prophetic preaching as squeezing people's cheeks till their teeth show, the way your mother did when you were a wiggly kid in church as she hissed in a stage whisper, "Behave or else!"

We cannot just tell people to be good or else. We've got to preach from the right mountain. Not Mt. Sinai, but Mt. Zion.

Prophetic preachers can seem like the church's gunslingers, the Clint Eastwoods of the pulpit. "Go ahead, make my day." But that's the problem. Me, I relate more to Clara Barton. She started the Red Cross.

We know that prophetic preaching is not all hard edged and flinty, but it is heavy, like stone tablets, and has the urgency of "no tomorrow," even when tomorrow is the point. It doesn't usually scratch where people itch so much as it finds ignored infections and applies holy medicine that stings.

All preaching should be prophetic in one sense, I suppose. But usually the phrase is more focused. Prophetic preaching is a voice crying in the wilderness or beautiful feet running with good news on a desert road. It is preaching stripped down to essentials, like John the Baptist with nothing but his camel-hair tunic. *God is holy. Christ died and rose again. Repent. Live righteously. Hell and heaven.* Like that.

Our models have fiery eyes, hoarse throats, and they don't always dress well. They have had it up to here with excuses and have no time for pleasantries. They are preachers who have paid a heavy price and are not about to get sidetracked into talking about leadership strategies or growing Sunday schools. They cry when they preach and pound the pulpit, if not their chests. They would not have been invited to pastors' conferences—no sense of humor—and they would not likely stick to the conference theme.

Awkward!

But this kind of in-your-face preaching poses something of a challenge for gospel preachers. How do you get up and preach, "Shape up or ship out," when the congregation has just sung "Jesus Paid It All"? Prophetic preaching so often seems to go to the dark heart of bad behavior just when our people have gotten used to hearing about "grace that is greater than all our sin." Prophetic preaching for us must be law tuned to grace.

One thing is for sure: Our prophetic preaching cannot be mere moralism. We cannot just tell people to be good or else. We've got to preach from the right mountain. Not Mt. Sinai, but Mt. Zion. Once we're at that grace place, where we stand with "Jesus the mediator of a new covenant," then the prophet can preach, "See to it that you do not refuse him who speaks" (Heb. 12:18–25).

In a strange twist (call it "the foolishness of God"), the potency of New Testament prophetic preaching is not in scaring the hell out of people. There is the urgency of *must* in prophetic sermons, but grace adds the beautiful countermelody of *able*. In Christ, you *can* do what God demands. Our preaching must be one way God fulfills his new covenant promise to write his law on hearts rather than stone. And grace is his pen.

Prophetic grace, however, is not only about forgiveness. Grace has backbone. So prophetic preaching outfits God's people with grace. Preaching alive with grace wrenches the remote control from people's hands, snaps off the computer and the coffee, and pushes them out the door to live like Jesus in this glassy-eyed world. Grace is what we're sent out to *offer*, without price, not just what we are forever *taking*. In prophetic preaching, we insist that God's people carry grace.

Stilts

Prophets, for all their differences, have some things in common. For one, you always get the feeling that God himself has come up on the platform and grabbed the microphone out of the preacher's hand. You can almost hear the feedback in the sound system. "This is what the LORD says," says the prophet, and we forget about him in order to hear God speak. I would hope that God is speaking in all our sermons, but there are times when a sermon seems to have another voice, when it almost feels like there is a Ventriloquist moving our lips, and we have nothing to say about it.

Prophetic preaching also seems often to be intrusive, bluntly barging into the discreet silence of polite society. The Old Testament prophets, at God's insistence, said, "We're going to talk about this whether you like it or not. The silence is killing you. This sin is not acceptable even if you're used to it. You cannot ignore the people I care about any longer."

The prophets, too, always had a faraway look in their eyes. Recently I came across the art of Cody F. Miller, who has an uncanny knack for capturing biblical characters in quirky, insightful paintings (www.codyfmiller.com). Three of the prophets he painted—Isaiah, Jeremiah, and Jonah—are all on stilts, seeing the world from a vantage point different from everyone else. His Isaiah also has a magnifying glass.

Most important, those prophetic preachers saw the bright form of Jesus Christ, far off in the distance. Peter tells us that they "spoke of the grace" (there it is—*grace*) "that was to come to you." Peter says that "the Spirit of Christ in them . . . predicted the sufferings of Christ and the glories that would follow" (1 Pet. 1:10–11). So to be prophetic, our preaching must stir a yearning *for* Christ and a vision *of* Christ. Peter further challenges us, "It was revealed to them that they were not serving themselves but you, when they spoke of the things that have now been told you by those who have preached the gospel to you by the Holy Spirit sent from heaven. Even angels long to look into these things" (1:12). We ought to preach about Christ in such a way that the old prophets would whisper, "Of course!" and the watching angels would be wide eyed.

Future-telling

From their high stilts, prophetic preachers insist that people absorbed with the present refocus on the future God has promised. In some circles eschatology has gotten a bad name. It is good and noble to explore the perichoresis of the Trinity but you had better steer clear of "rapture" or "tribulation" or "the Rider on the white horse." It can come off as the trailer trash of theology, all lurid speculation, the Bible's "olde curiosity shop." But prophets, while certainly not having the end figured out, "searched intently and with the greatest care" (1 Pet 1:10) in trying to understand the future God promised in Christ. Our prophetic preaching should make room for some searching with great care. We do them a disservice if we pay less attention to their visions than they did. We will certainly not understand all the mysteries of Daniel, Zechariah, or Revelation, but how is it that some preachers have never preached *any* of them?

Prophetic preaching today needs to stand on stilts sometimes and look off into the future to the Second Coming, to the new heavens and new earth, and, yes, to hell. The future God has promised sounds a unique warning to complacent or sinful people who might not hear any other alarm.

But even more important than the warning to the complacent is the hope God's saints so sorely need. Christians—at least *young* Christians—may not think all that much about heaven, but God's people need to know all that God says about the future he has planned for us. They need biblical details, not just a sanctified version of "pie in the sky by and by." Prophetic preaching gives God's people an ear for the voice of the archangel and the trumpet call of God. It gives anxious disciples Jesus' word, "Do not let your hearts be troubled. . . . I am going there to prepare a place for you" (John 14:1–2). Prophetic preaching takes Christians fixated on the week ahead to a high place from which they can see, with John, "a new heaven and a new earth," and hear the voice that says, "Look! God's dwelling place is now among the people. . . . There will be no more death or mourning or crying or pain, for the old order of things has passed away" (see Rev. 21:1–4).

All of this is what makes preaching prophetic. While some "prophetic preachers" are really just irritable or angry—they're venting, like pulpit vigilantes, taking the law into their own hands—true prophets in the pulpit have "prayed through," as folks used to say. God has warmed their hearts and words. Something is different. Whereas on other Sundays these good preachers came with the Lord's medicine or a watering can or bread, on this Sunday God has given them a searchlight and a bullhorn. They clear their throats and discover they have "a voice of one calling in the desert, 'Prepare the way for the Lord, make straight paths for him'" (Luke 3:4).

Lee Eclov is the senior pastor of the Village Church in Lincolnshire in Lake Forest, Illinois, and a featured preacher for PreachingToday.com.

WHEN GOD IS REVEALED,
KNEES BOW

Mark Driscoll

Preaching isn't for wimps. According to Mark Driscoll, prophetic preaching is an unrelenting assault on spiritual strongholds. And everyone has strongholds, those thick walls that block us from experiencing Christ's presence. Driscoll exhorts preachers to use God's Word as a blunt weapon that attacks and dismantles those strongholds. It's not an easy task, but whoever said that war is supposed to be easy? Even so, as you read this short chapter, you'll also catch Driscoll's infectious joy about preaching. It's the joy of watching God work to take the walls down and set the captives free. In the end, that's worth the fight.

An expository sermon that exceeds an hour seems like a foolish way to reach postmodern people. Yet Paul tells us that though our message and our method (preaching) are foolishness, God uses them that he might get the glory.

Mars Hill Church is a postmodern church with an average age of less than thirty. We've grown to more than two thousand in attendance. With other leaders I've cofounded Acts 29, a peer-to-peer network that has planted churches throughout the United States and around the world.

We've discovered that all the hype about experience seeking is not true. Postmodern people aren't seeking experiences; they're seeking God. And the point of preaching is to unveil him. An experience is a shadow of God, the visible result of a person's encounter with Christ, not Christ himself.

If we chase after experiences with all the candles and labyrinths and trappings of postmodern worship, we merely chase after shadows. But just as the primary point of Scripture is to reveal God, so the primary point of expositing that Scripture is to reveal Christ.

In studying a passage to preach, I ask three questions:

- Who is God?

- How is he revealed in this text?

- What are the most natural inclinations that resist or deny that truth?

Then, for the rest of the sermon, I seek out that resistance and break it.

If God is revealed as holy, why do we resist his holiness? Because we don't want to think of ourselves as unholy. If Scripture reveals Christ as sovereign, why do we resist his reign over our lives? Because we don't want to surrender. These are the strongholds that preaching assaults.

Preaching is unique in its power to break people. And once broken, once softened, God rebuilds repentant lives.

I have seen hundreds of people broken by a single sermon. I love to see people reach the end of their pride, autonomy, and self-reliance. This is what inspires me to preach: watching broken people bowed in repentance, hands extended to receive Communion, and then those same hands lifted in gratitude and praise.

Mark Driscoll is the preaching pastor for Mars Hill churches, the cofounder of the Acts 29 Church Planting Network, and the author of numerous books, including *Death by Love* and *Vintage Jesus.*

PART 2

The Craft of
Prophetic Preaching

A NEW KIND OF URBAN PREACHER

Timothy Keller

For more than thirty years, Tim Keller has been preaching and watching God change lives in an urban, skeptical, postmodern context. What's his secret? In essence, Keller's prophetic preaching is based on two simple convictions. First, preach the gospel. Keller just keeps offering the truth of Scripture, the beauty of Christ, and the wonder of God's grace. The gospel changes hearts and transforms cities.

Second, Keller also tells preachers to understand their cultural context. Keller practices this all the time. He listens to his parishioners. He understands what they deal with at work or in their homes. He reads the thought shapers of postmodernity. He watches films and reads fiction.

He exemplifies how we can avoid "tribal preaching"—a style of communication that resonates only with fully convinced believers. Keller challenges preachers to understand their culture's "alternative narratives." In other words, understand your listener's worldview (or story), Keller urges, and then winsomely present the new life offered by Jesus. Since Christ alone can meet the deepest needs of our hearts, people in our culture are already hungry for Jesus anyway.

As an example, in his book Counterfeit Gods *Keller wrote, "To contemporary people the word idolatry conjures up pictures of primitive people bowing down before statues." Notice how Keller communicates that he understands and sympathizes with his hearers' assumptions about the biblical teaching about idolatry. For Keller, prophetic preaching doesn't mean that you must go out of your way to offend and irritate unbelievers. In this interview Keller provides some practical insights on how to preach the gospel while engaging your unique cultural setting. In the end, whether unbelievers agree or disagree with your sermons, they can still leave feeling respected, understood, and perhaps at least one step closer to Jesus Christ.*

What part has preaching played in shaping a different sort of urban Christian at Redeemer Presbyterian in New York City?

The Sunday preaching has been pivotal for two reasons. It has provided the basic idea of what it means to be an urban Christian—its definition, why the city is important, and why being a Christian in a city is important. However, preaching is also a way of modeling for people. The preacher is *being* an urban Christian. Preaching is a way of showing that the preacher is processing and assimilating the urban environment. I, as the preacher, interact with books, magazines, ideas, and issues that everybody else in New York City is interacting with.

I often will put forward and interact with statements by non-Christian New Yorkers who have problems with Christianity, and I'm modeling how you should interact with and help your friend who doesn't believe in Christianity. So I'm not just giving people information about how to live as an urban Christian; I'm actually being the urban Christian in front of them, and being one in such a way that they can envision being that themselves.

Can this be practiced whether preaching in Manhattan or in a small town in the Midwest?

Yes, the weak Christian, the nominal Christian, and the non-Christian have to be able to say: "I could see myself being a Christian like that person." If you are preaching, and your audience is learning truth, but they could never imagine being like you—responding to the world like you, thinking like you, and feeling like you—that's not good. This is important regardless of the setting.

You've said that we need to build a countercultural community where sex, money, and power are not used in destructive ways. What part can preaching play in building that sort of community?

A biblical theology of sex is neither the prudishness of the traditional culture nor the commoditization of sex in a consumer culture. When you're preaching, instead of simply saying, "Here's what the Bible says about sex," it's your job to contrast Christian sexual ethics and practice with what's out there. It's important to say, "In the world today, here are the alternative narratives that people are using to understand sex."

Give illustrations. Quote magazines. Give illustrations from movies. You have to say, "Here's what the Bible says about sex," but you also have to say, "Here's what the culture says, and it's different."

I have to do the same thing with money and power. I not only have to expound positively what Scripture says, I also have to show that I understand, even sympathetically, the strengths and weaknesses of alternative accounts—and what those accounts are, because there are usually more than one. I have to show people that I live in their world; I know what those alternative accounts are and how Christianity and the Bible's approach are different.

In this sense I follow Abraham Kuyper and the Dutch Calvinist approach. They would say that any account of sex, money, or power that isn't God centered makes an idol out of sex, money, or power. And there are different ways of doing that: In a traditional culture marriage is the idol. In our culture it's the sexual experience itself. But if you make anything an idol, it leads to destruction. When you make a good thing into an ultimate thing, it leads to destruction.

For example, if I love my child, that's a good thing. But if I make an idol of my child, so that I'm either living my life through my child or favoring my one child over another child, that leads to destruction. It leads to breakdown.

You must identify the particular way the culture makes idols of sex, money, and power. Show how they lead to destruction, and show how it is only when you demote sex, money, and power by sticking them into a Christian account of reality that they are no longer destructive.

You say that Christians should be a community radically committed to the good of the city as a whole. How does your preaching at Redeemer bring good to the city at large?

If preaching is really confusing or offensive to non-Christians, then that preaching is pretty tribal. If it's confusing or offensive because the preacher is just not careful about how he says things, he's not showing that he remembers what it's like not to believe. And a lot of preachers do not give their hearers the impression that they have any idea what it's like not to believe or to have doubts.

Some preachers with a liberal bent like to talk about the doubts they struggle with to make doubters feel welcome. I don't think that helps doubters much, because the preacher is not leading them. Some people of a more conservative bent preach as if doubts are the worst thing in the world: Who in their right mind would ever doubt? And how dare you doubt!

There is a way of expressing the verities of the faith with love and assurance, yet also in a way that shows you respect people's doubts and remember what it's like to doubt. Verse 22 of Jude says, "Be merciful to those who doubt."

If you've got that attitude and voice as you preach, you become a place where non-Christians can come. And even though they don't believe what you believe, they're edified, interested, and helped. You'll have swarms of non-Christians who are able to leave—sometimes challenged, sometimes not agreeing—but almost always intrigued, provoked, and edified. And it becomes the whole city in a church rather than just you Christians.

It is possible to preach in a way that includes Christians and non-Christians, so that you have a lot of non-Christians present, incubating, listening. That becomes a way of lifting up the whole city instead of just your tribe.

Completely aside from the offense of the cross, how can preaching turn people away?

You can preach the truth wrongly. There is a way of saying, "If you reject the truth, you're lost, and this lostness goes on forever," in which the preacher almost relishes that. There are preachers who clearly relish that, or if they do act sorrowful, it doesn't come across as genuine. They're just glad they're on the right side of the doctrinal divide, that they're not lost.

The *spirit* of your preaching may not be right. I may not find anything wrong with what you're saying—I believe it—but there's something about the spirit that is hard edged and, for non-Christians in particular, difficult to relate to.

I see this in some preachers who say they believe they are sinners saved by grace, but they don't act that way. They act like people who believe God is pleased with them because their doctrine is right and they're living the life they ought to live and they're really sold out for Jesus. That attitude comes through in everything they say.

The truth is the truth, and generally the truth is difficult for non-Christians to hear, but the preacher's spirit goes a long way in whether or not people can see that he is sympathetic, really cares about them, and really loves them. Conversely, people can sense a spirit of "here's the truth, and I know you're not going to like it, and that's okay by me because it's the truth." If we tell people the truth, and the heart, voice, and attitude are full of sympathy and humility, the hearer recognizes that.

Even when we are talking about morality?

Let me give you an example. I could just say, "The Bible says this, and we have to accept it because the Bible is the Word of God." Or I could add: "Now, for some of you, I know that sounds outrageous. That sounds like 'take it or leave it.' But I'd like you to consider this and this and this."

If I give an aside and ask them to please consider this, they see I respect them and know they may have trouble with it. Even though I'm not giving in to anything, it shows I know they're there.

Whereas if I give no further explanation than to say, "The Bible is the Word of God," and I just keep on going, what I'm communicating to them is: *And what idiot would doubt that the Bible is the Word of God? All sane people know the Bible is the Word of God.*

I don't believe that. I'm a Calvinist, and because I'm a Calvinist, I realize belief isn't something people can work up without God's help. So why should I preach as if I think anybody who has any trouble believing what I'm saying is an idiot? It should make me compassionate with those who doubt.

You've talked about the importance of training people to go into their workday world to help develop humane, creative, and excellent business environments. How do you shape your preaching at your church to train people to accomplish this?

I throw in illustrations. If I'm talking to actors or people in business or in the arts, and I get some insight as to how the gospel would affect their art or their business, I try to find some way to work it into a sermon. Sometimes it's stretching, because that isn't directly helpful in elucidating the text, and I'm an expository preacher. What I do, actually, is write these illustrations on a piece of paper and stick them in a pile. Every week, as I'm preparing a sermon, I pick them up and see whether they fit.

The other possibility is occasionally finding time to preach a full sermon on integrating faith and work, and then I could use all the illustrations directly.

You've said that the church can attract people to Christianity by showing how Christ resolves our society's cultural problems and fulfills its cultural hopes. How does your preaching do that?

In 1 Corinthians 1, Paul says: The Jews want miracles and the Greeks want wisdom, but Christ is weakness to the Jew and foolishness to the Greek; yet to those Jews and Greeks who are being saved, Christ is the wisdom and power of God. Paul is saying that the essential, cultural hope of the Jews was finding something that works—power. The cultural hope of the Greeks was wisdom—speculation and philosophy. So there were different cultural narratives, and Paul confronts with the cross the idolatry of each culture. Paul says Jesus is the ultimate power to the Jew, and he's the ultimate wisdom to the Greek.

In the end you will attract people by saying that the narrative story lines of their lives will find a happy ending only in Christ. In a way you are affirming them. It's okay to look for wisdom; it's okay to look for power.

Go after people; get to know their deepest hopes. And after you've confronted their idolatry, show that, in Christ, these deepest needs will be met. At a certain point, you do have to say, "If you're longing for identity, love, freedom—or whatever your cultural narrative is—it's in Christ that you will find that longing satisfied in the truest way."

If you really know your audience, there's always some part of Jesus' teaching that will resonate with them: Jesus as bridegroom, for example, or liberator. It depends on your culture, but some aspect of what Jesus is doing is going to be incredibly attractive to it. You have to find out what that is and hammer it as often as you can.

Timothy Keller is the senior pastor of Redeemer Presbyterian Church in New York City, and the author of numerous books, including *The Reason for God, The Prodigal God, Counterfeit Gods,* and *Generous Justice.*

THE UNCHANGING GROUNDS
OF OUR AUTHORITY

John Koessler

Why should I listen to you? Whether we like it or not, some people start asking that question before we even finish our sermon's introduction. We could bristle with defensiveness, or we could follow John Koessler's advice: Address the question—honestly and biblically.

So how do we reach people who may not trust us? How do we preach to a skeptical, antiauthority culture? Koessler urges us to avoid two common extremes in preaching. The soft approach says, "I have no right to meddle in your life, so I'll just share my personal experiences." In contrast, the tough approach says, "This is God's Word, so listen up and deal with it."

Both extremes miss the mark. Preaching is the proclamation of God's Word, but it's also a form of two-way communication. It's not just what you say; it's how people hear what you say. So effective preachers boldly proclaim God's Word, and they win the hearts of their listeners. The apostle Paul followed this pattern, declaring God's Word and connecting with his listeners. We'll avoid Paul's example at our peril.

As Koessler warns, "It's almost impossible to listen to someone you don't like." In other words, we can proclaim God's truth all day, but if we exude impatience, arrogance, or disdain for our listeners, they'll smell it a mile away and tune us out. When that happens, we can preach our hearts out but nobody's listening.

Key questions about authority in preaching

Authority in preaching can be a controversial topic. Who gives me the right to stand up and make pronouncements about God and people's personal lives? When it comes to preaching with authority, there are three basic questions we need to address:

- Do I have authority to preach?

- Where do we locate a sermon's authority?

- Is this notion of authority outdated?

The first question—Do I have authority to preach?—is being asked on both sides of the pulpit. The listener wants to know, why should I listen to this guy? But the preacher today is also asking that question. We live in an age where there is a lot of challenge to authority. As a result, there has been a shift away from the idea of authoritative preaching. With the younger generation, there is discomfort with preaching from a position of authority, and so now you have talk about approaching hearers with a more humble orientation in a conversational model of preaching.

If we decide that preaching does have authority, then the second question comes into play: Where does that authority come from? Traditionally there have been three places that people have located authority. One is in the preacher's office. You should listen to preachers because they are the authorized teachers of the church. This idea is especially prominent in the Catholic churches.

Things shifted during the Reformation. For Luther and Calvin, the authority is located in the message itself. Why should you listen to the preacher? Because the preacher preaches the gospel. If the preacher's message does not conform to the gospel, then you don't have to listen to the preacher.

In the modern era you have a loss of confidence in the text. The location of authority is in the experience of the listener. That's where we are today. You can see this, though, decades ago in a figure like Harry Emerson Fosdick, who said that the main objective of the preacher is to address some particular need or problem in the life of the audience. When listeners identify with the problem and see that the preacher is addressing it, that gives the preacher authority. It's a pragmatic approach.

So authority is based in the listener's experience of the message. If the message works for the listener, it has authority. If it doesn't work, even if the person up front is preaching the Word of God, listeners don't regard the message as having authority.

You hear the third question—Should we even care about authority today?—in the "emergent" conversation. They're not approaching the audience from the point of view of dogmatism. It's not a proclamation; it's a conversation.

The emergent pastors aren't the only ones to have approached it from that point of view, though. Decades ago Fred Craddock wrote the book *As One Without Authority*. He argued for a different model of preaching, moving away from a deductive, proclamation-based approach, to a more inductive, audience-focused approach. You try to draw the audience into an experience. The weight is placed on the experience of the listener, and that's what validates the preaching.

How listeners respond to a preacher's authority

Listeners don't have an inner debate on it; they just tune out. When someone is listening to you for the first time, you probably have about a four-minute window at the beginning of the message when the listener is making a judgment about whether you have credibility. It's not a question of *where did he go to school?* or *is his theology straight?* The listener's assessment is often rooted in ethos, the sense they have of the person who's up there preaching. It is very experiential. They're gauging the preacher by nonverbal cues and by the issues the preacher is raising.

That happens every time we preach; people make judgments about it. So for the listener, that question is a question of validity. For the preacher, it's a question of confidence. Where is the basis of my confidence to stand before these people and address the most intimate issues of their lives? For example, let's say there's a couple that's been in a committed, nonmarried relationship for seven to ten years. They happen to wander in, and in the course of my sermon I say, "If you are living together outside of the covenant of marriage, what you're doing is wrong; you need to change." Well, what gives me the right to say that? That's really a question of authority. Where's the basis for my being able to address them—not just in the moral issues of their lives, but on eternal questions. For me to say, "You're going to heaven; you're going to hell," that stems from questions of authority.

The authority of preaching is always derived authority. It's never innate to the person. There's this issue of position. How do I think of myself as a preacher? Well, I think of myself as somebody who was commissioned by God, somebody who is commissioned by the church. That gives me a certain level of confidence. But the validity of that comes from the message, the fact that what I am preaching is the Word of God.

But preaching is not just about what is said. It's tempting for me as a preacher to stand before the audience and say, "Look, I'm here on God's behalf. It doesn't matter whether you like it, and it doesn't matter whether you like me. The only thing that matters is what God has said, so deal with it." There's a certain personality type that seems to go along with that. It's sort of appealing.

But the truth of the matter is that if I don't have any concern for the audience, they're going to reject what I say. Preaching isn't only a matter of what is said; it is also a matter of how it is heard. So I do have to ask myself: How does what I'm saying impact the listener? Am I addressing the questions they came with today, the needs they have, the objections that arise in their minds as they listen to me declare the Word? If I don't speak to any of that, I'm not going to be able to preach with authority.

You see all three of these aspects of authority reflected in Paul's preaching. First, there's a positional location for his authority in that he preaches as an apostle, a commissioned messenger of Jesus Christ. There's a story about George Whitefield preaching to a crowd, and he notices a man up front who is starting to doze off. Whitefield slams down his Bible, and the guy jerks awake, and Whitefield says, "Oh, I woke you? Good. I meant to, because I come in the name of the Lord of Hosts, and I demand a hearing because of that."

Second, for Paul the nature of the message is critical, so he warns the Galatians: "If anybody comes to you and preaches a different gospel, let him be cursed" (see 1:8). For him, the validity of the message is also in the nature of the message: Does it agree with what God has said? This is the prophetic test of preaching. If you envision the preacher standing in the tradition of the prophets, God's Old Testament people were told to test everything that the prophets said, and if a prophet said anything that disagreed with God's revealed Word, the people were to reject it.

Third, Paul has a deep interest in his listeners. You see it in the way he is in a kind of dialogue with those to whom he is writing. He will raise their questions—"some of you will say"—and then he'll answer them. You see it in those moments when he exposes his heart and talks about his own concerns. Paul does not just tell them the message; he tries to win them over. You see this particularly in the Corinthian letters where there is this deep anxiety over the way the Corinthians are hearing and perceiving him. It's important to him as a preacher to have an eye on the way his audience is listening to him.

Two extreme positions on authority

Today as we're trying to sort through this subject of authority in preaching, we have a tendency to move to extremes. One extreme is to say: People don't relate to authority today, and, besides, who am I to stand up and tell people what they should think or do? So I'm just going to share my experience. I'm going to tell you what it looks like from where I'm standing, and we'll have a conversation about this.

That's one extreme. The other extreme is the attitude that everything I'm preaching to you is right, and therefore if you disagree with me, well, you can come up and apologize later, because I agree with God. It doesn't matter what you think about what I say or who I am, because this is what God says, and you just need to come to terms with that.

The problem with both of those extremes is that preachers will most likely miss a large part of their audience.

The Reformers struck the right balance. Their understanding was that the preachers' authority comes from the Word; because it comes from the Word, they can stand before anybody. We can stand before kings; we can stand before the common laborer; and we can make statements about what God expects—not because of who we are or our role in the life of the church, but because we are presenting what God has said.

This doesn't mean that preachers shouldn't show their humanity and their personal experience. People grant preachers authority often based on what they know of the preachers' experience. Again it's a matter of ethos. People are often asking, what kind of person is this that I should listen to him? In sermons from thirty years ago, there was little personal sharing done by the preacher. In such cases it often portrayed the preacher in a parental role where they were setting a good example. For the preacher to stand up and expose a flaw is a contemporary preaching practice.

Although sharing personal stories may help build trust with the audience, it can also be a trap if the sermon becomes an exercise in narcissism in which I'm primarily talking about myself. There needs to be some balance. The model is the apostle Paul. You see his transparency in what he says about his own fears and past experience. He describes his movement from Pharisaic Judaism to faith in Christ and how wrong he was before that move. At the same time he's not afraid to stand on his calling as someone who's authorized to speak for Christ.

The modern audience doesn't want to hear just a doctrinal construct in the message. They want to know something about the preacher, and particularly they want to see the humanness of the preacher. But in my personal opinion, I'm getting tired of hearing self-absorbed preaching. It seems that we've swung too far in that direction. We have this genre of preaching where the center of the message is the preacher. All the illustrations revolve around personal experiences the preacher has had. It has a self-absorbed quality to it that I find myself reacting against. I would like to see the pendulum swing more to the middle. In my own preaching I'm probably more reserved in my use of personal illustrations than I was ten years ago.

The experiential model of authority also has an element of what I would call not so much pragmatism but dynamism. It is similar to Karl Barth's approach to preaching. For him the validating element in the sermon is what God does with it. It's not even so much the biblical text. The authority is in what God does as the preacher declares the biblical text, and the Holy Spirit comes and makes it the Word of God to the listener. How do I know this is authoritative? Because of what God did as I was listening to it. This is a factor in the way people listen to sermons today.

These are the two tests of authority for the audience today: (1) Is the preacher saying anything that applies to where I am? (2) Did I experience God while the preacher was speaking?

The push for "conversational preaching"

In the contemporary church there are voices pushing for a more conversational or dialogical approach to preaching. They advocate for a communal basis for authority. In describing this approach, Brian Larson at PreachingToday.com uses an analogy from bowling. The preacher serves as the bumpers you put in the gutters when kids are bowling. The preacher just makes sure the church doesn't go too far right or left as the church works out its views on the truth.

But once again, that gets back to where we locate the seat of authority. My main argument against this view is that when you look at the New Testament and what it says about the church's responsibility with respect to what is declared, the authority for preaching is never placed in the community. The authority grows out of what God has said. Christ declares the Word; he delivers it to the apostles; the apostles deliver it to the church; then the church has responsibility to preserve what has been handed down to them. Their role isn't to say, "Let's all get together and decide what we're going to believe about this." There's an element of tradition here, so Paul describes the church as the pillar and the foundation of the truth. Paul is saying the church upholds the truth. The church has been given this deposit of authoritative truth, and it is responsible to proclaim it and to preserve it. Paul also says the church has been built on the foundation of the apostles and prophets, and that implies a doctrinal foundation of what the apostles and prophets are teaching. So I think that those who say the authority rests in the community have got it wrong. The authority is anchored in the Word that has been given to the community.

I recall hearing one of the leading voices for dialogical preaching in a conference, and he was asked, "If you're going to engage genuinely in dialogue with people, don't you have to put everything on the table?" That is, don't you have to put every doctrine on the table and at least hold out the possibility that you could be wrong about things like the deity of Christ, the substitutionary atonement? As I recall, his answer was, "Yes, if you're genuinely going to engage in dialogue, you have to put everything on the table and say I might be wrong about that."

I find that extremely problematic, particularly from the point of view of someone who is responsible to proclaim the core of biblical truth. In the New Testament, when you look at the various terms used to describe what happens when preaching takes place, behind the language is this implication of authoritative declaration. I'm not speaking for myself, and there's this body of truth. It's not a conversation.

Also, on a practical level, we need to debunk the idea that the younger generation always reacts negatively to someone who speaks with authority. Some high-profile preachers have a strong sense of authority and a strong following among younger people. How do we explain that?

Ethos is always a factor. Part of what people respond to is the person. It's very hard, almost impossible, to listen to somebody you don't like. If listeners conclude that the preacher is conceited or doesn't care about them, it's an uphill battle for the preacher. So there is an element of ethos; there are people in every generation who respond to an authoritative personality. The names I hear that a lot of our students love to listen to are James MacDonald, John Piper, Mark Driscoll. So there is a significant population responding to this proclamation model, this declarative model.

Preaching authority or authoritarian preaching?

What's the difference between a preacher's authority and authoritarian preaching? Again, that goes back to ethos. Preaching with authority has to do with my confidence in the basis for my message. I am confident that I have a word from God and that the reason you have to listen to me is because this is what the Lord has said. Authoritarian preaching, on the other hand, is a personality type. That's preaching as bullying. You have to listen to me because I say you have to listen to me. Authoritarian preaching is often reflected in a dislike for the audience. One of the questions listeners unconsciously ask when they hear a preacher is, *does the preacher like me?* (Or, *if the preacher knew me, would the preacher like me?*) In the first few minutes of the sermon, you can sense when preachers are embittered toward their hearers. Authoritarian preaching doesn't have anything to do with authority.

There's a kind of narcissism reflected in it. It approaches the audience from a utilitarian point of view. There's something I want to gain as a result of your response to my message. The authoritarian preacher doesn't care about the legitimate questions the listener has. There's no compassion in it. Still, not every preacher who ignores the questions of the audience is an authoritarian preacher; some are just insensitive.

Titus 2:15 says, "These, then, are the things you should teach. Encourage and rebuke with all authority. Do not let anyone despise you." That's a critical verse for the issue of authority in preaching. Authority has to do with the content of what Titus declares—that he is a messenger of the living God who declares God's Word. It reminds me of what Whitefield said: "I come in the name of the Lord of Hosts, and I demand a hearing because of that."

Authority is an issue for both sides of the pulpit. For the audience it's a question of validity; for the preacher it's a question of confidence. I really do have to know what right I have to stand before this audience and address the most fundamental issues of their lives, to meddle, really—to stand before them and talk about their affections, values, moral decisions, their marriages, and their children. I'm telling them how to live; where do I get off doing that? Every preacher has to answer that question. The only answer is to trace back to where you get your message from.

The only thing that gives me the right to do that is what I say accords with what God has said. I am declaring his Word.

John Koessler is the chairman of the pastoral studies department at Moody Bible Institute in Chicago, Illinois, the general editor of *The Moody Handbook of Preaching,* and the author of *A Stranger in the House of God*. He's also an editorial adviser to PreachingToday.com.

THE THREE KINDS OF PREACHERS

James MacDonald

Teacher, shepherd, prophet—those are the three "primary colors" of the preaching world. Teachers impart knowledge; shepherds offer comfort; but prophets challenge our rebellion against God. Although every preacher will gravitate toward one gift (James MacDonald clearly prefers the prophetic role), we need to mix all three gifts into our preaching ministry.

With this clear and practical outline, MacDonald challenges us to prayerfully consider our personal preaching gifts and tendencies. What is your primary preaching gift? Where do you feel most comfortable? If you're only a prophet, or only a shepherd or teacher, how can you grow in the other preaching gift areas? How can you become a well-rounded preacher?

There are three kinds of preachers: the teacher, the shepherd, and the prophet. Teachers have things they want you to know. I thank God for people with the gift of teaching. You need to know about God, the atonement, his Word, victory over temptation, the power of the Holy Spirit. We need teachers. (My wife tells me she wants to learn something in every message, so I try to teach!)

The shepherd is the caregiver. While teachers are consumed with the mind, shepherds focus on emotions. They want to comfort, encourage, and strengthen their flocks. Every message should do that.

The third kind of communication giftedness is the prophet. While the teacher is concerned about the mind and the shepherd is concerned about the emotions, the prophet is concerned about the will. The prophet says the reason you're falling short of God's will is not that you don't know enough, and it's not that you're just discouraged. The problem is not ignorance; it's not discouragement; the problem is rebellion. You don't want to do what God wants you to do.

Though I try to balance these three primary preaching gifts, I definitely operate most often as a prophet. That's the dominant expression of giftedness that the Lord has entrusted to me. I'm going to challenge the will of my listeners. I'm trying to motivate people to make a decision to do what they know.

In contrast to my gift areas, John MacArthur is a teacher much more than a prophet. Chuck Swindoll is a shepherd. He knows how to encourage people.

So you have teacher, shepherd, and prophet—mind, emotions, will; or ignorance, discouragement, rebellion. But we have to be careful, because we tend to think that everyone needs what we do best. I constantly work at developing the shepherd and teaching components of my preaching ministry. That also derives from my pastoral vision, which involves staying at the same church for my whole life. Thus I need to become well-rounded as a pastor. On the other hand, it's hard to hide your primary gifting.

It's important that we celebrate all of these gifts rather than looking suspiciously at other preachers, wishing we had this gift or that gift. All of these gifts are essential for building the church. What happens when you rebuke ignorant people? You crush them. You're telling them "just do it," and they don't even understand what they're supposed to do. That's hurtful. What happens if you rebuke a discouraged person? That person just gets more discouraged. Many preachers understand that intuitively. But what happens if you teach a rebellious person? That person just gets more rebellious! So you really need all three components. You can't afford to neglect any of them.

It's like parenting. We may try to comfort our kids when they're rebellious, or we try to teach them when they're discouraged. You've got to assess the situation and ask the Lord for wisdom, because those who are rebellious need to be rebuked, and those who are ignorant need to be taught, and those who are discouraged need to be encouraged. Many times all three problems are mixed together, so I try to have all these elements in my sermons.

James MacDonald is founding and senior pastor of Harvest Bible Chapel in Rolling Meadows, Illinois, a radio speaker for *Walk in the Word,* and the author of numerous books, including *God Wrote a Book* and *When Life Is Hard.*

CHALLENGING HEARERS

Lyle Dorsett

There's one thing that preachers can't do: They can't beat the world at being worldly. But that simple truth opens the door for Lyle Dorsett's concept of prophetic preaching: Don't offer people the world; instead, use God's Word to offer them a beautiful alternative in Christ. Then when people get tired of the devil's lies, they can start the journey back home to God the Father's house. In this sense prophetic preaching stirs up a distaste for the "far country" of sin and a hunger for our new life in Christ.

Like all of the authors in this volume, Dorsett believes that prophetic preaching is practical. It might move us to tears or make us squirm with conviction; but it also leads us to take specific steps as we follow Jesus. Of course the preacher better take those steps before he or she asks anyone else to do it.

For Dorsett the life-changing power of prophetic preaching hinges on one word: anointing. It refers to those who trust God to unleash extraordinary power through their ordinary personality. How does a preacher get the anointing? We don't earn it; God anoints us as we allow the Holy Spirit to be preeminent in our lives.

In this wide-ranging interview, this veteran preacher and professor opens a treasure trove of wisdom on prophetic preaching. As you learn from a wise guide, may God's anointing fall on you.

What is your theology for challenging hearers when you preach?

I believe that when we do preaching we're called to challenge people. We're called to exhort people and encourage them to take specific steps to become more Christlike. First John 2:6 says that if we abide in Christ and he abides in us, then we will walk as he walked. And in that epistle as well as in Peter's epistles, there's a call to holiness, a call to Christlikeness, a call to walk as Jesus walked, with Jesus as the head of the church.

So one of the things a pastor should do is encourage the flock to take steps to confess sin, to truly repent of that sin, and then make a commitment to practice a life of following Christ. I'm very intentional about that. That's exactly what happens over and over again in the exhortations found throughout the New Testament. People are being exhorted. Paul would often encourage, admonish, and reprimand his readers.

So our preaching should take the same form as the epistles of the New Testament in terms of getting down into the nitty-gritty and working with people?

Too often people see preaching as just teaching, but if it doesn't have a component of exhortation and challenge that calls people to change, to grow in Christ, or to take purposeful steps to build the kingdom, it's not really preaching; it's only teaching. You can exposit the Epistle to the Ephesians for several weeks and help people understand what's in the text and what's being said there, but if there's not application with a challenge to apply it, you've had teaching but you haven't had preaching.

What influences have shaped your practice of challenging people?

My life has been changed by some of the challenges and exhortations I've received from good preaching. I'm a midlife convert. I was living in Boulder, Colorado, and commuting to Denver, and one of the things that brought me to Christ was listening to a local radio station on the sixty-four-mile round trip every day. As I drove I would listen to my favorite radio preachers who constantly fed me. They also gave me a consistent challenge: Do something about this and take a step. And some of those things have had such a profound impact on me that I've never escaped them.

In particular, I remember one of my favorite radio preachers saying, "Many of you believe you need to dumb down your youth programs and entertain your youth, because you're afraid you'll lose them if you don't try to imitate the world. We can't imitate the world. We don't have the resources. The world's got more money. They're better at the world than we are. And you need to hold the line firm. Yes, you want to be relevant, but you need to have a church that is a genuine alternative to the world, so that when some of your youth go out and rebel—and many of them will—and when they've had enough of the world, they have a genuine alternative to return to."

I've never forgotten that. That's what I want in our church. We may offend people. They might leave. But when they're sick of the promises the devil has made about how glorious this life-style is going to be, when they know it's bankrupt, they have an alternative to come to rather than a cheap imitation of what they already tried and found wanting.

How would you describe your own challenges in preaching?

I don't have a set pattern, but generally in a sermon I'll take my text and talk about the context—who it was being written to, how they would have seen it and heard it and understood it. Then I'll point out the spiritual principles. After I look at that, I'll say, "Now what do we do with that today?" So I'll have an application with a challenge to do something.

Last Sunday I preached on the Magi visiting the holy family, and I focused on Joseph. We looked at his context and how he was trying to walk faithfully with God. But he needed to hear from God. He had all these confusing problems. And God spoke to him. I was trying to get the church to see that God is going to speak to you if you're trying to walk with him. He'll even give you a dream if you need one, to show you what to do. He will not let you go to the wrong place. But you need to begin with Scripture. You need to be a person steeped in Scripture and to know the Scripture and hear God through Scripture; and then if you need to know whether to go to this school or that school or to take this trip or that trip, he'll let you know. As long as you're not in rebellion, he won't let you go to the wrong place. He'll block you. You can count on that.

Then I challenged them. At the end of the service, I gave them Robert Murray McCheyne's Bible calendar, which I use. It takes you through the whole Bible every year, and the New Testament and the Psalms twice. I said, "I want to challenge everybody in this church to use Robert Murray McCheyne's Bible calendar this year, because you need to be in the Word." Then I laid out three things we're supposed to do when we read the Scripture:

- Read it devotionally to be inspired and fed.

- Read it as a lamp unto our feet to guide us, to show us how to deal with things.

- Read it to get the mind of Christ.

Everybody received one of the Bible reading calendars in the order of service. I said, "Take this with you and prayerfully consider using this, because you need the mind of Christ. You need the guidance of Scripture. You need to feed on it devotionally. So let's get into this together."

So you give exposition, and then you give application?

Yes, I give a contextualization of it, an exposition, and I outline some principles. Then I give an application and a challenge. But I never challenge people to do things I'm not doing or won't do. How can I ask my congregation to tithe if I'm not tithing? We've got a building fund for our church. I can't challenge them to give to the building fund if I'm not giving sacrificially to the building fund. As preachers we have to have integrity. The fabric has to be integrated between what I tell them to do and what I'm doing or willing to do.

A number of years ago, I was working on a biography of A. W. Tozer, and I talked to a man who worked with Tozer as associate pastor and youth pastor for three or four years when he was in Chicago. I said, "What did you learn from A. W. Tozer? Tell me some of the things that changed you." He said, "One of the most important things I learned from Tozer was to never preach a text you haven't lived or that hasn't lived in you."

That takes you beyond, I know the Koine Greek, and I'm going to teach you this text. Instead, as preachers we need to ask ourselves: Has this text exegeted my soul? Or am I merely exegeting it? There's a world of difference between knowing about Scripture and actually living it. So I try to pray for a couple of weeks in advance, *Lord, let this text live in me somehow.* Sometimes that ends up being painful, and I'll have to do something because God answers that prayer. But then I can honestly say to the congregation, "Join me in what's in this text."

As Paul wrote in the Epistle to the Ephesians, "I pray your love may abound more and more in knowledge and depth of insight. I pray that the eyes of your heart may be opened" (see Eph. 1:17–18; Phil. 1:9). These verses show that our hearts have to be circumcised. The Scripture is a two-edged sword. It should come in and circumcise our hearts.

Talk about how you would define anointed preaching and how that relates to being a preacher who challenges people properly.

Martyn Lloyd-Jones has a book called *Preaching and Preachers.* Chapter 16 of that book is on the sacred anointing. It's a mystery. Billy Graham was anointed. Billy Graham has had a phenomenal evangelism gift. You can't describe it. It's not that he was so technically good or this or that. This man had an anointing. The Holy Spirit called him out, set him apart, and anointed him. Corrie ten Boom was that way as an evangelist.

This is a mystery, but it says in Ephesians 4:11 that some are called to be evangelists, some are called to be prophets, some are called to be apostles, and some are called to be pastors and teachers. The Spirit sets people apart; he anoints them. And if he anoints them, there will be power.

And sometimes God withdraws his anointing from people. For instance, in the book of Revelation, Jesus tells the church at Ephesus that they're good at pointing to the sin of other people and they do wonderful Christian activities, but they've also lost their first love. Then he goes on to warn them that he will remove their candlestick.

That's the withdrawal of the anointing. The anointing is the presence of the Spirit, where the Spirit is working.

I pray, *Lord, feed me so I can feed my flock. Teach me so I can teach my flock.* He knows my people better than I do. He knows what they need. I don't. I have a responsibility to try to know these people—to know who's got cancer, who's just learned their daughter has run away, who's learned his wife is terminally ill, who's lost a job—but the Holy Spirit of God knows what they need; I don't. So I say, *Give me what they need, please.* That's the anointing.

And when the anointing is present, you can't help but be challenged.

Exactly. Sometimes you think you're anointed, and you may not be. You may just be high on caffeine. And sometimes you think maybe you're not anointed, but God honors those who honor him. If we're faithful, if we ask him to give us what his people need, he'll do it. That's what the anointing is all about. It is his work, not ours. We must cooperate and study our text. We have to do our homework and we have to preach, but it's got to have the additional emphasis from the Holy Spirit. The illustrations must come from him, and the nuances must come from him. The way you end up approaching the text, even the challenges, has to come from the Spirit. That may sound mysterious and ethereal, but it's got to be that way. Otherwise it's me thinking, *I know this stuff. I can exegete this text. Therefore I will teach these things.* Yes, you want to be able to do that, but most of my congregation doesn't give the skin off a grape what the

Koine Greek says about this text. They're crying out, *I'm dying. Is there any balm in Gilead?*

What are the soul issues of the preacher that can lead to effectiveness or ineffectiveness in challenging hearers?

We have to study and show ourselves approved unto God as workers that need not be ashamed. And we have to tend to our own souls. When we step into a pulpit on Sunday, we are what we've been all week long. If we've been involved in a secret sin during the week, we carry that into that pulpit. We are what we feed our minds and our souls on. If we're not in the secret place with the Lord, if we're not with him and hearing him, letting him feed us, we have nothing to give except our own stuff. Romans 8:8 says, "Those who are in the flesh cannot please God." That applies to preachers.

A century ago F. B. Meyer used to say, "There are three kinds of Christians out there. Christ's Spirit is present in everybody who's born again; Christ's Spirit is prominent in some people; Christ's Spirit is preeminent in, alas, only a few." Where does that preeminence come from? It's from feasting on the Word, reading devotional literature, being in prayer, being filled with the Lord rather than watching garbage television or dissipating your time shopping or whatever else it might be.

This doesn't mean that we don't have a life outside of our preaching role. We have to have a life that's outside of being in the secret place, so to speak. Nearly fifty years ago, the British writer Evelyn Underhill put it so well. She was giving a talk to Anglican spiritual leaders, and she said that most people will come to a pastor so they can take an instant journey into the distant country of the supernatural and spiritual maturity. Of course these instant-results people don't live there most of the time, and yet they show up on Sunday or they come to your office and they need help. They're like an English tourist who visits Germany. They don't know the language. They don't know the country. They need somebody who knows the language and the country to be their tour guide and show them around. At any given moment, most of the people in your church are like that English tourist. But you know the language of the host country; you know how to get around; you can serve as their tour guide; you can lead them to the places they need to see.

We have an enormous responsibility and a great privilege. But it's part of who we are; it's not just part of what we study.

When I think of the people who have most challenged me, certainly the specific steps or challenges they give have a place, but what challenges me the most is their intensity and commitment to Christ, their love for Christ. That challenges you no matter what they talk about.

That's right. This is our clear focus: to become the person in whom Christ's Spirit is preeminent. People have said you have to spend an hour studying for every minute you preach. That's impossible for me; I don't have that kind of time. I do think you need to study a lot before you preach. But you also need to be on your knees and hearing the Lord and walking intimately with him, because he knows what those people need more than you do, and he'll let you know.

When have you challenged people from the pulpit or heard an instructive challenge from another preacher?

About two years after I'd become a Christian, a preacher challenged me to get through the whole counsel of Scripture every year. He said that you can never be a soul physician and care for souls if you don't know the Scripture. And you need to know the whole counsel of Scripture. A man who doesn't know his Leviticus and Numbers is malnourished. So from that time on, I started my yearly Bible reading pilgrimage. I made a commitment to read through the whole Bible every year devotionally, and it changed my life.

In early October I gave a sermon at our church. I felt the Spirit was leading me to preach on spiritual depression, because increasingly I find people who are suffering from what used to be called melancholia. They're depressed. At Wheaton College, where I taught, we had one counselor when I came in the early 80s. Now we have a whole team of counselors. The line to the counseling center is enormous. We have a culture that creates more and more hurting people. And I believe the Holy Spirit can do something about that. I know every *body* does not get healed on this side, but I do believe Christ wants to heal every *soul* now.

So during that sermon I said, "I know many of you are suffering from depression. I too have battled that over the years. But Jesus Christ wants to heal you, and I have some spiritual prescriptions for the healing of the soul. I want to offer you a challenge to try some of these spiritual prescriptions during the next week." Then I said, "Follow up with me and let me know what's working. If what you try doesn't work, let me know, and we'll try something else. It's as if you have an infection and you try amoxicillin but it doesn't work, so you then try a 'big gun' like Cipro. We'll do that with the spiritual things. We'll give you a prescription."

So I offered a challenge of one or two prescriptions. Then I said, "Please let me know whether this is working." I've never had a sermon where so many people responded. It was phenomenal. People were e-mailing, or they were calling to say, "I've been doing this, and it's working." One woman said, "I've had bad dreams for three years since my mother died. I'm trying thus and so now, and it's working." I say praise the Lord.

What problems have you run into with challenging hearers? What have you learned you have to watch out for?

One size doesn't fit all, and the things that have worked for me don't necessarily work for others. I used to preach all the time, "You need to be up early in the morning, like Jesus in Mark 1:35, and go into the quiet place to read the Scriptures and pray. How can you take on the world without doing this?" Then some nice women who were more mature than I said, "Lyle, if you had four kids at home, and your husband left to catch the train at 6 a.m., you wouldn't be going off in the quiet place like Jesus early in the morning. Surely there's got to be another way." I thought, *I can't believe I've laid that on these people this long. God forgive me for this arrogance of assuming that everybody will come to Christ like I did, or that everybody will be touched by the Holy Spirit like I have been.*

George MacDonald once said, "Let the Holy Spirit be as creative in how he works with the next guy as how he worked with you." More and more I see that people don't come to Jesus the same way. There's not a neat little pattern for how people come to Jesus or for how people get freed of this or challenged to do that. So I'm trying to speak and preach and teach with authority but at the same time not be so certain that I know the only route of how this works. I'm not saying all roads lead to a deeper relationship with God. But I want to work more on hearing from the Spirit, letting him tell me how to work with this soul.

Do you think a church can be overchallenged?

Yes. Sometimes my wife says to me, "Lyle, you give them too many challenges. They can't handle them all." So I try to back off. It's a matter of balance. That's why I say there may be a number of applications in the text, but it doesn't mean they're for everybody. I will usually have a challenge at the end of the service, at least to pray about something. But I can't say to them every Sunday, "Start doing thus and so," because they don't have the same calling I have and they don't have the time or energy for all of this. Even though we're all called to grow into Christ's likeness, we're not all going to grow at the same pace or with the same disciplines.

Do you feel there are times when the primary purpose of a sermon should be to convey truths about God and the Christian life but not necessarily call people to climb the mountain?

The purpose of every service is for people to enter the presence of the King of kings. They need to meet Jesus. This coming Sunday I'm preaching on the baptism of Jesus, and I'm doing eight baptisms. The text talks about the heavens opening up and the Spirit of God pouring down. I want them to experience that and see that as these little ones are baptized—the heavens opening and the Spirit pouring down. That's not a challenge to go do anything, but it's a challenge to receive that and celebrate it.

So not every challenge is a "go and do."

No. Sometimes it's a "receive and be."

That's the biggest challenge right there—to be.

It's not always "go do" or "stop doing," but sometimes it's "be." Sometimes it's "be open and allow God to work." We have Holy Communion every Sunday, and sometimes I just challenge them. I say, "On the road to Emmaus, in Luke 24, this is the first Holy Communion we know of after the resurrection. Jesus breaks the bread and gives it to them. They eat the bread, and their eyes are opened. Taste and see. Come to the Lord's table today and ask him to help you see."

Lyle Dorsett holds the Billy Graham Chair of Evangelism at Beeson Divinity School in Birmingham, Alabama. He is pastor of Christ the King Anglican Church and the author of numerous books, including *The Essential C. S. Lewis, Seeking the Secret Place,* and *And God Came In: The Extraordinary Story of Joy Davidman.*

APPLYING AND PREACHING FROM THE OLD TESTAMENT PROPHETS

Andrew C. Thompson

Sometimes we really can't see the forest for the trees. That cliché makes a good point: Sometimes life requires that we back up and get the big picture before we plow forward. In this chapter Drew Thompson takes us on a theological helicopter ride, providing an aerial view of the entire forest of prophetic preaching.

He begins with a simple question: How do we preach from the Old Testament prophets? Thompson cautions us not to impatiently grab five principles from Hosea's ministry or nine principles from the life of Jeremiah and then make them apply to our lives. Those are "tree questions." Instead, we should get some altitude and survey the entire landscape so we can ask a "forest question": Where and how do the prophets fit into the story of God's covenant with his people?

Getting this larger, forest view isn't always easy. It won't provide a simple, one-size-fits-all answer for every prophetic text. It will also make the preaching process a little longer. Sure, it's quicker to stay on the ground as we plow through the trees; but in the long run, that quick approach only narrows our perspective. Thompson's theological overview of the prophets will help us interpret these biblical texts in their own context. Once that work is done, we can proceed with confidence to apply the prophetic messages and predictions into our lives. Although this approach forces us to work a little harder, in the end I think you'll agree that it was worth the ride.

For many preachers, though the rest of their Bibles may be well worn and underlined, the section after the Song of Solomon and prior to Matthew remains in mint condition, gilded edges still gleaming. How can we bring this section—the Old Testament prophets—into the pulpit? How can we help our people become familiar with those strange men of Israel and Judah who felt God's words like a fire in their bones?

Traditionally there are two paths available to anyone who wants to preach from this section: First, the preacher can trace a prophecy of Scripture and its eventual fulfillment in history (Figure 1). The lesson is usually that the Bible is true, or that God keeps his word. But fanciful guesses and speculative end-times scenarios haunt this road. Besides, one often wonders in these types of sermons—where is my audience in this text?

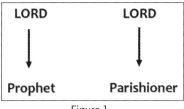

Figure 1

More commonly preachers can focus on the sections that tell a story about the prophet's life. Here the preacher draws parallels between the life of the prophet and the life of the parishioner (Figure 2).

But this approach also suffers from disadvantages. In the first place, it is individualistic. The Holy Spirit inspired Isaiah to

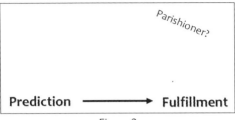

Figure 2

create a masterful account of his calling and God's glory in the temple (Isa. 6:1–8). Did God do this just to provide a blueprint for how he might call Joe Smith to a pastorate in Cincinnati? This passage probably has a grander purpose. Second, it can be wildly inconsistent: it applies some details of a narrative (like Jonah's running from God) to modern lives and omits others (huge storms, giant fish, Assyrian hostility, God's care for livestock, predicted disaster, and miraculous vines and worms) in a manner that seems suspect. Finally, it can drastically limit a preacher's selection, since most of the prophets' writing is *not* narrative in form. Most sections are "prophetic speech," to use a phrase of Claus Westermann—oracles from God to his people Israel, through the mouth of an inspired prophet.

In this chapter I want to outline another way forward for applying and preaching the prophetic passages of the Old Testament. By focusing on the *covenant context* of a prophetic speech, preachers can apply such a passage to their own churches in richly textured ways that are faithful to the biblical author's intent while being helpful for building community.

Prophetic passages in the Bible

The prophet shares God's message with those around him. But this revelation from God does not take place in a vacuum!

These are not just any people to whom the prophet speaks. They are Israel—the LORD's own nation by covenant. They are bound to him and to one another in an intricate web of relationship, to which the prophets refer again and again (Figure 3).[1]

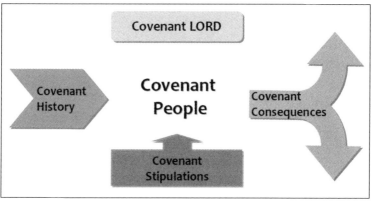

Figure 3

Prophets speak about Israel's covenant LORD, whose character forms a basis for their relationship (Isa. 44:6–8). They talk about their history with him and his faithfulness in the past (Ezek. 16:1–14). They remind Israel of the requirements of their covenant with God (Hos. 10:12) and how they have or have not kept them. And they repeat the covenant consequences of blessings for obedience and curses for rebellion (Isa. 1:18–20). Often a single passage runs through several of these phases in turn. In Micah 6, for example, under the guise of a lawsuit against his people, God reminds Judah of how he brought them into the Promised Land (6:3–5), discusses the type of response he

---

[1] The term *covenant* here acts as a unifying motif for all the aspects of God's relationship with Israel. It does not necessitate a "covenantal" view of theology. See below for a discussion of how theological differences may impact one's use of this model.

requires (6:6–8), observes their faithlessness (6:9–12), and warns of curses to come (6:13–16).

Figure 3 can apply to any of the covenant arrangements that were in effect during Israel's history. The Abrahamic, the Mosaic, and the Davidic covenants were the primary arrangements depicted in the Old Testament. Prophets drew on each one as appropriate, since each covenant carried its own stipulations and consequences. In fact the vast majority of prophetic oracles follow this pattern, highlighting one or more of these covenant elements. This was their standard model.

Applying the prophets to the church community

In *The Modern Preacher and the Ancient Text,* Sidney Greidanus notes that in applying biblical passages to our audience, we should usually resist the comparison between the biblical *character* and the modern *audience*, drawing life lessons from the experiences of biblical characters as the main thrust of a passage.

A stronger comparison can be made between the biblical *audience* and the contemporary *audience*. In other words, the wise interpreter will not ask, "How are my people like Hosea?" but will instead ask, "How are my people like the people to whom Hosea preached?"

The fact of the matter is that Hosea was unique. The preacher may find it difficult to separate what was true *only* about Hosea (e.g., his calling, his character, his ministry, and his marriage) from what can carry over to modern listeners. These choices then become arbitrary, based on what we as preachers want to say anyway. So we might use Hosea to encourage marital fidelity, but not to justify marriage to prostitutes.

On the other hand, Hosea wrote to the average Israelite. Our audience and Hosea's are alike in that *they are audiences.* Comparisons between audiences will proceed on much safer grounds than comparisons between prophets and audiences simply because the two groups have so much more in common. So the prophets' words primarily apply to the church at large (as God's covenant people) and to the individual Christian as a member of the church.

Our new covenant context

As Figure 4 indicates, New Testament believers also live in covenant with God—what Jeremiah 31:31 calls a "new covenant." This new covenant is made under the authority of the covenant LORD, in the light of his past deeds for their good (salvation in Christ), under his demands for love and obedience, and in the hope that God's promises of salvation and judgment will be fulfilled at the return of Christ. This similarity provides the surest bridge for applying the prophets today, as the words of the prophets to the Old Testament community are applied to the New Testament community.

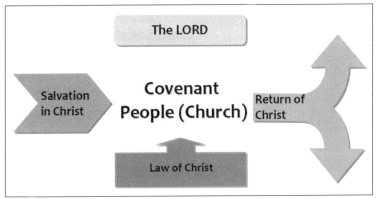

Figure 4

Of course appropriate application will also take into account the differences between Israel and the church, between the old and new covenants. Much of what the preacher makes of these differences will depend upon the theological system to which he or she subscribes. Some will posit more discontinuity between the covenants, either by drawing a sharp distinction between Israel and the church, or by labeling the old covenant "conditional" (a ministry that produced death) and the new "unconditional" (producing life by the Spirit). Others may see more continuity between the two. How one understands the redemptive situation in Israel and in the church will guide the application and preaching from a prophetic oracle.

Relating their context to ours

The Scriptures record a string of covenantal arrangements between God and his people (Figure 5). Each covenant has its own place in redemptive history; ours comes between the cross of Christ and the return of Christ, and as such has unique features that must be reckoned with when seeking to apply old covenant principles in a new covenant situation.

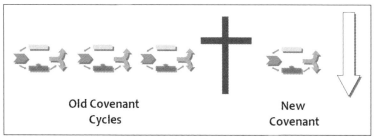

Old Covenant
Cycles

New
Covenant

Figure 5

This model for application takes each part of the covenant arrangement (God, history, demands, and promises) and asks how it relates to the respective aspects of the new covenant.

Their Lord is our Lord. The easiest connections to make are when dealing with the messages that discuss the character of God (which never changes). This is a case of strict continuity between Israel and the church. Isaiah 40:12–31 speaks of God's tremendous wisdom and power, displayed in creation and in his sovereign rule over the nations. He is not to be compared with idols or with any human power. That idea will preach in any church today!

Their history may be our history. Sometimes the prophets recall God's promises and saving acts on behalf of his people that directly apply to the church. Consider Micah 7:18–20, where the prophet recalls God's promises to show steadfast love to Abraham and Jacob. These promises provide the basis of assurance that their sins will be forgiven. The New Testament is clear that the promises to Abraham are given to those who are in Christ (Gal. 3:29). That part of their history is also our history, and we can count on God's forgiveness and love, even when confronted by the enormity of our sins.

On the other hand, sometimes the redemptive "distance" between the prophet and the church calls for a more indirect approach. For example, Hosea 11:1–4 recalls God's kindness to Israel in the wilderness and their response of unfaithfulness. Many preachers and theologians would not see the exodus as "our" history, since that event occurred under the Mosaic covenant. However, the New Testament repeatedly applies exodus imagery and themes to Christ's life and to our own redemption from sin and death (see, e.g., Matt. 2:15; Mark 1:2–3; Rev. 15:2–4). Since Christ has redeemed us with mighty acts of judgment and salvation, we have an exodus of our own to recall and for which we should give thanks.

Their demands may be our demands. Some covenant demands for righteous behavior translate easily. Micah (6:8) calls us to do justice, love mercy, and walk humbly with God, while Hosea (4:1–14) rails against murder, lying, stealing, cursing, and adultery. Jeremiah (22:13–30) condemns injustice and greed. All of these passages find clear parallels in the lives of our parishioners who are still under the injunction to "be holy, for I am holy" (Lev. 11:44; 1 Pet. 1:14–16).

On the other hand, Malachi demands tithing, while Haggai exhorts his people to build a temple. Again, depending on theological perspective, the distance may be too great for a straightforward application. As Haddon Robinson advises in *Leadership Journal* (Fall 1997), one should move up the ladder of abstraction, deriving increasingly general principles from specific demands, guided by scriptural parallels. So Malachi's tithing may translate to sacrificial and joyful giving (see 2 Cor. 8). Or Haggai may encourage us to build up the temple of the church (which becomes people and not a building [1 Pet. 2:4–5]) or to put God's priorities ahead of our personal comfort (Luke 9:23–24). Either the prophetic demands are directly applicable to our situation or a more general principle can supply the parallel.

Their promises may be our history. At times, what was future for the original audience is now past for us. The promises and warnings that God gave the prophets have already come to pass. So when modern readers see God threatening to destroy Jerusalem in Amos 3:11–15, that word is not directly a threat for us, since ancient Jerusalem was destroyed in 586 B.C. Instead, we can think of the message as it must have been preserved for the exiles that lived through the destruction of Jerusalem. Amos 3 explains why God's people have suffered so much, highlights the seriousness of God's wrath, and guarantees the coming of the judgment that he still has in store at the return of Christ.

When Isaiah spoke of a future restoration from exile (43:1–7), which is past from our perspective, we can thank God for keeping his word and caring for the faithful remnant, and we can reflect on how God continues to protect his people in the midst of suffering and trials.

The preacher should also note that some of the prophets' messages seem to be partially fulfilled, as today we live in the "already but not yet" tension of the new age. A preacher can work from Joel 2:28–32, where God says he will pour out his Spirit freely on his people. This happened at Pentecost, and we can be grateful for God's past action and presence by his Spirit. However, the latter part of this prophecy, that

> "The sun shall be turned to darkness
> and the moon into blood
> before the great and awesome day of the Lord comes."
> (Joel 2:31)

has not yet come to pass—we still await the final judgment.

Their promises may be our promises. Finally, what was future to them may still be future to us. We can preach from Zechariah 14 about the coming time when God will visit his people, splitting the Mount of Olives in two, saving them from their enemies, and making the entire land "holy to the Lord." Or we can talk about the coming of the Son of Man on the clouds in Daniel 7, when he receives the kingdom from the Ancient of Days.

Of course one message or book may contain several of these phases. Consider, for example, the book of Joel. The prophet depicts a locust invasion (past for both Israel and us), an actual invasion of an army (future for Israel and past for us), the pouring out of his Spirit after those days (future for Israel and past for us), and the valley of judgment on the day of the Lord (future for Israel and for us). Some of these words point to their past, some to their present, some to their near future, some to the new covenant mission, and some to the coming rule of God on earth (Figure 6). We should be aware of how each of these elements applies to our own situation.

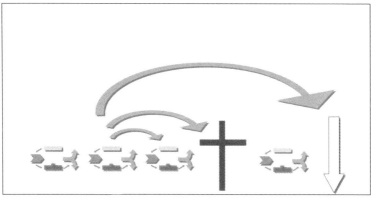

Figure 6

The point of all of these examples is to show how the predictions of the prophets remain relevant for our day.[2] Instead of drawing tenuous parallels between prophets and individuals in our church, or between Israel and our nation, this approach relies on the much broader base of a shared communal identity as the people of God.

This approach will give the preacher more material to work with, since most Old Testament prophetic passages fit this description. It can also bring confidence in application, because it provides consistent criteria for an interpreter.

---

[2] The following are two additional examples of sermons that follow this basic approach: Al Fasol, "Preaching from Malachi," *Southwestern Journal of Theology* 30 no. 1 (1987): 32–34; Timothy M. Pierce, "Micah as a Case Study for Preaching and Teaching the Prophets," *Southwestern Journal of Theology* 46 (2003): 77–94.

Finally, this model can help to build a community's identity. Too often our people look into the Bible to find (only) themselves. Of course God's promises and warnings and declarations do affect our day-to-day lives, our most minute decisions, and the inner thoughts of our hearts. But (especially in the prophets) they address these realities from the perspective of being a member of a community that is in relationship with God. As parishioners learn that this wonderful Lord and his gracious promises come to them because they are part of the church, their membership in it will become more central to their self-understanding.

The prophets were not isolated individuals, and neither are we. We are all members of a community that is bound together by thick theological cords. Those cords not only connect us to the present, but by memory they reach back into the past, where God has proven himself in mighty deeds of salvation and judgment. By hope they also stretch into the future, where God will usher in his glorious kingdom in a climactic manner, making all things new. These cords provide the bridge from their time to ours.

Andrew C. Thompson has served as pastor of Mt. Carmel United Methodist Church in Henderson, North Carolina. A ThD candidate at Duke University Divinity School, Thompson writes a bi-weekly "Gen-X Rising" column for the *United Methodist Reporter* and is editor of *Generation Rising: A Future with Hope for the United Methodist Church.*

PREACHING FOR REVIVAL

Anne Graham Lotz

How would you describe the spiritual state of the American church? In this chapter Anne Graham Lotz claims that we've become complacent, cold, backslidden, and anesthetized. It's not a pretty picture. All the signs of our culture point us toward one glaring need: revival.

Based on Lotz's study of revivals throughout history, they often begin when we hit bottom—individually and corporately. In other words, we don't build up to a revival; it starts when we're desperate. God can use the honest desperation of one Spirit-hungry person who begins to pray and preach for revival. That one preacher doesn't make revival happen; he or she merely serves as the mouthpiece for the Spirit to sweep through the land like a mighty wind, renewing the church and transforming society.

So prophetic preachers are always asking: How do I get out of the way and let God speak? Lotz doesn't focus on preaching techniques (although she does provide a simple outline for preparing a sermon); instead, she gives a stirring call for preachers to bathe their efforts in prayer. Thus she urges preachers to "pray in preparation; pray in proclamation; pray in postscript." It's our job to pray and proclaim Jesus; it's God's job to send the mighty winds of revival in his time and in his way.

A burden for revival

In the past few years, the Lord has been placing a burden on my heart to preach for revival. I did a series on revival several years ago at The Cove, the Billy Graham Training Center. Before doing the series I was convinced in my own mind that we were living in the last of the last days of human history. Based on that assumption, I didn't think the Bible prophesied that we would have revival in the last days. Instead, I thought the Bible prophesied that people will gather to themselves teachers who will tell them whatever their itching ears want to hear, that there will be a falling away from the truth, an apostasy in the church. So I didn't have a vision for revival.

But in my study of the Scriptures, I came across various passages that I felt could predict a time of refreshing and revival before the Lord comes back. Now I feel God giving me a desire from his Word to bring revival. Of course I want to experience it first in my life, but then I also want to bring it to others through the teaching of his Word, which he's called me to do. Sadly, many of us have gone to sleep, and I want to see God awaken the church in its relationship toward him.

Let me explain what I mean by revival. First of all, you can't revive someone who is dead. I'm referring to someone who has already placed their faith in Jesus but perhaps has grown complacent, cold, backslidden. Our lives are busy and filled with other things. In America in particular there are many distractions to maintaining a sharp edge of commitment to Christ. All the material prosperity in our country has anesthetized us to our need. We just don't feel the need for Jesus, for prayer, for God's Word as we do when life gets hard.

Revival is an awakening in our relationship with God where we place him first—first in our thoughts, first in our time, first in our activities, first in the way we spend our money. We make him the priority of our lives.

In Wales, Ireland, England, Scotland, and even in America, there's been the history of revival that's usually begun on the part of one person who has started to pray and had a burden for revival. As God puts that on the one person's heart to pray and then begin to share his Word, God sends his Holy Spirit in such an overpowering way that people repent of their sin and return to the cross of Christ. They are cleansed and filled with the Holy Spirit. It impacts the church. The church comes alive in their love for Christ, in their heart for the gospel, and in their love for a lost world.

The second thing that happens is evangelism on a broad scale. Because of what takes place in the church, people all through a community and region can receive Christ because of the impact they've seen on the church.

The third thing that takes place is an impact on society where crime drops and social issues are righted. People treat their fellowman as God commands.

The fourth thing that happens, interestingly enough, is persecution. People who have placed their faith in Christ become so obvious in society that the devil raises up his people to persecute them.

God has honored, historically and biblically, several ingredients for sending down revival:

- Prayer
- The preaching of his Word
- The exaltation of Jesus Christ

Then it's a Spirit thing. Jesus said in John 3 that the Spirit of God is like the wind, and you can't control it. You don't know where it's coming from, you don't know where it's going. You know when it passes through. You see the evidence of it, but the Spirit of God is the wind of God. Revival is something God chooses to do. I'm praying with all my heart that he would choose in my time to send down the wind of the Holy Spirit in a fresh way, that the church might be awakened, that the bride might get ready, because I believe we're living at the end of human history.

The signs that precede revival

It's interesting what signs precede revival. The church is in the worst condition it's ever been—totally apostate, drifted from God's Word. Society is at its most decadent. Revival is not something you build up to. It's when everything is about the worst and most hopeless that you could see. I feel our country, because of prosperity, is blinded to the moral and spiritual bankruptcy that has come. That is evidence that we are desperately in need of revival.

I see also within the church, generally speaking, in all denominations, a falling away from God's Word. I see a substitution of entertainment and all sorts of secular and practical means of drawing people into the church. This is a substitution for a real movement of the Spirit of God. Prayer meetings in church are poorly attended, if churches even have them. If they have them, then they dress them up with all sorts of musicals and things to draw people in. People don't just come to pray anymore.

I also see the hearts of people hungry for something. We're seeing that in the new spirituality. People are looking for something to fill that spiritual void. The tragedy is they're looking for a God they can make up, one they're comfortable with. They're not turning to the God of Creation, the God of Abraham, Isaac, and Jacob. They're turning to a God that is a conglomerate of what makes them feel good. The message of the Christian church seems to be silent. We try to accommodate those people and draw them in without clearly presenting the person of Jesus Christ.

So a lot of ingredients are in place for God to send real revival. In our ministry we focus on Jesus. We focus on the Word. We try to keep our focus no matter where we go, what we do. And I find that people respond.

The role of preaching in revival

Preaching that leads to revival is always faithful to the Word of God. There's no substitute for biblical exposition. God speaks through his Word. When we give a topical message, we read a text, and then we talk about the text, and often what we're saying about the text is not God speaking. Pastor Steven Olford once told me, "Anne, if you get up and take a text and pull in other things and give illustrations and whatever, then that's what Anne Lotz says and nobody cares. But if you take a passage of Scripture and break it down so that you're opening up that passage of Scripture, God speaks and everybody wants to listen."

So my aim in speaking is to take a passage of Scripture and free God up to say what he wants. When I approach a passage of Scripture, I'm not trying to force into that passage what I think the audience needs to hear. I don't think about my audience and what I think they need. I take a passage of Scripture and ask God to unveil for me what he says in that passage. Then I try to deliver faithfully what I feel he's saying through that passage.

In my mind's eye I see God in heaven having so much he wants to say to his people and to the world, but we often attempt to put a muffler over his mouth. We're his spokesmen, and he wants to say something, and we actually have a hand over his mouth because we're saying what we want to say. Maybe what we say is based on truth and there is nothing false about it, but God speaks through his Word. We remove the hand from over his mouth when we take a passage of Scripture and let him speak freely and clearly through his Word.

Second, revival comes from preaching bathed in prayer. We can get up and give a clever expositional message with an outline—and it can be cold as ice. A Scripture passage is clothed with the power of the Holy Spirit through prayer. I'm talking about prayer and fasting when you prepare the message. I'm talking about having people in your congregation who are committed to pray for you as you prepare the message and when you deliver it.

The place of prayer in preaching

Prayer should be the single most important aspect in our preaching. I always begin with a very simple prayer: "Lord, help me." Then before I even open my Bible, I ask God to speak to me because I want to hear his voice speaking to me personally. When I approach a passage of Scripture, I always begin by approaching it personally and devotionally. I read a passage and take a few verses and ask myself, what does it say? I list the facts. Then I ask, what does it mean? I try to find the spiritual lesson from those facts. And then I ask myself, what does it mean to me? I take the lessons and put them in the form of a question I would ask myself. Again and again I have heard

God speaking to me through a passage of Scripture. As God speaks to me through that passage, my heart is warmed, and my mind is opened.

Then I go back and take that list of facts and break it down into an outline. I come up with an aim, what I think the passage is saying, and I phrase it to cause the audience to do something specific. When they hear me give the message, I want them to take action. It is not an action I've thought of; it's an action that comes from the passage of Scripture. Then I go back and rework my message in keeping with that aim so God can speak his aim through that Scripture.

I pray before I study. I pray during study. Often I can't come up with the outline, and I pray until it unfolds like a flower. Then I go back and pray the sermon through. *God, does this make sense? Is this what you want to say?* I pepper it with applications, questions I would ask the audience, and I ask God to give me those applications. Then I pray when I finish the sermon, going back through it before I get up to speak. I put it down before God and get on my knees, and I pray it through. I ask God to help me crucify myself so that I would have no awareness of myself, no self-consciousness, and no agenda except to give clearly and faithfully the message I believe has come from his Word. Then I just release it to him.

Sometimes in the pulpit he brings to my mind things I hadn't prepared. I'm well prepared at that point, so I don't really talk off the top of my head. But he does bring applications, things to my mind that I hadn't thought of before. I want to be free in him to give what I feel he puts on my heart.

And then when I finish preaching, I practice a lesson I learned from Elijah when he went up on Mt. Carmel. After he prayed and God sent down the fire, he wasn't finished. He went back and got on his face to pray for the rains to come. And he prayed until the rains fell.

Based on Elijah's example, after I walk off a platform, I'm still not finished praying. I have to pray until the rains come. Sometimes the rains come when the people are on their way home. So I've told my prayer team at home not to stop praying when I finish. They pray for a month after I've spoken that the fullness of God's blessing will fall on those who heard that message. After I've spoken, as the message sinks in, as people begin to apply it, that's where the blessing of God falls. We have to pray in preparation; we have to pray in proclamation; then we pray in postscript that God would fully bless what we have faithfully delivered.

Our role versus God's role in preaching

But that doesn't mean that revival comes on our timetable. Ultimately revival is up to God. The response of the audience is God's responsibility, not ours. You don't have to stay on revival themes. According to Jesus himself (see Luke 24), all Scripture speaks about him. As a result, you can preach the whole counsel of Scripture and exalt Jesus. John Stott said that a good Bible expositor ought to present Jesus in every message, because Jesus is in every passage of Scripture. You can preach through the whole counsel of Scripture and still be exalting Jesus. You can preach through the whole counsel of Scripture and bathe it in prayer.

We don't have to call people to brokenness; we don't have to call people to repentance. If you preach God's Word faithfully, God will bring people to repentance. God will convict them and bring them to brokenness. At the revivals we're leading, I don't preach on revival. I lift up the cross and the resurrection and the throne of Jesus Christ, and then I expect him to bring the conviction and for him to stir people's hearts. If we're preaching the whole counsel of Scripture and taking people through a portion of Scripture, I think increasingly we create a hunger for God's Word.

Anne Graham Lotz is the founder and director of Angel Ministries, based in Raleigh, North Carolina. She is author of several books, including *Just Give Me Jesus* and *The Magnificent Obsession.*

HIS WORD IN YOUR MOUTH

Kenneth Ulmer

Every preacher knows that preaching can wear you down. It's hard work. Studying the passage, getting that big idea, praying it through, writing the sermon, delivering it, listening to critiques and comparisons, and then starting the process all over again on Monday—sometimes it feels like slogging through a neck-high muddy swamp.

But Kenneth Ulmer reminds us that God wants to raise preachers up. In this chapter Ulmer preaches to the preachers and speaks prophetically to the prophets. He bases his encouragement on two bedrock biblical convictions: (1) God is a God who speaks and (2) God wants to speak through you—even the most "ordinary" preacher in the most "ordinary" setting. So when it feels like that swamp is up to your neck, Ulmer tells preachers, "God sovereignly chose you as his mouthpiece." Remember and rejoice in this: The God of the universe reaches down into the mud, lifts you up, and blesses you as he tells you, "I have put my words in your mouth."

Ultimately it doesn't matter if you're preaching to thousands or to a dozen. Ulmer keeps pointing to the miracle behind every preacher's call: God wants to use you, even despite your flaws and weaknesses. Once that sinks into your mind and your bones, Ulmer says, you'll never preach the same way again, and you'll never stop thanking God for his amazing grace.

Jeremiah 1:4:

Then the word of the LORD came to me, saying:
"Before I formed you in the womb I knew you;
Before you were born I sanctified you;
And I ordained you a prophet to the nations."

Then God says in Jeremiah 1:9: "Behold, I have put my words in your mouth. See, I have this day set you over the nations and over the kingdoms." God says: I formed you. I sanctified you. I ordained you. And I set you over the nations. But before all of that, I knew you.

And then God says five words that will change your life: I put *my words in your mouth.*

God says to the prophet: I knew you before you got here. Before I formed you, I knew you. Ephesians 1:4 says God *chose* us before the foundation of the world. The word means "to speak out." God says: I spoke you out before the foundation of the world. He says: I *knew* you. The word implies an intimate relationship: I knew you intimately. I knew you before you were formed in the womb of your mother. And then I set you in place. I sanctified you, called you aside unto myself. And I ordained you.

You are where you are on purpose. God does not move by accidents. He moves by providence. And he has providentially ordained and assigned you where you are today. You are not there by accident. You are not there because some committee voted on you. You are not there because denominational strings were pulled. You are there because God has set you in place, and he set you there that he might be glorified in and through you. And one of the ways he does that is to place his words in your mouth.

God is the God who speaks. He is not a silent God, as the idol gods were. God spoke to Abraham: Get out of here and go to a land I will show you. He spoke to Moses: Go and tell Pharaoh I said, "Let my people go." When Jesus spoke, it was said of him that never a man spake as he spake. The Holy Spirit spoke and told the young church to separate Paul and Barnabas and send them out. The Bible says: Let him who has ears hear what the Spirit says. And God says that you as pastor, you as shepherd, stand before the people of God with his words in your mouth.

The Bible says of Elijah: He was a man of God. Elijah said: Thus saith the LORD. So he was a man of God with the Word of God, and he stood before the people of God. So you stand as one with the Word of God in your mouth for the people of God. And you stand in the world created by God. God says he has placed his word in your mouth. He says to Jeremiah: I touched your mouth, and I put my words in your mouth.

God entrusts his word to my mouth

Several revelations come forth from that declaration. When God says he put his words in my mouth, it suggests, first of all, that God *entrusts* his word to my mouth. Jeremiah realized being one who speaks the Word of God is an awesome task, so Jeremiah, as many of us do, resisted and began to wrestle with God. He talked about how unqualified he was. Moses did the same thing. Moses was used mightily by God and only had two things—a stutter and a stick. But that which he spoke from his mouth was the very words of God.

God says to you, pastor, that he has placed his words in your mouth. Not his voice, but his words in your mouth through your voice. So when you stand to speak the Word of God, you speak not your words but his word, because he places his word in your mouth. It's his word, your mouth, through your voice. So when you stand on Sunday, when you stand on Wednesday, when you stand to minister, you speak with your voice, his words. When you stand to speak his words with your mouth in that house at that time, God sounds like you.

He does not say he puts his *thoughts* in my mouth. He's already settled that: "My thoughts are not your thoughts" (Isa. 55:8). I'm not asking you to handle my thoughts. Your motherboard does not have enough memory space to hold all that I would speak to you. You'd blow a fuse, and your mind would automatically delete some stuff. So I'm not trying to help you to think my thoughts. If you can just speak my words. I speak my words through you, because I entrust my words into your mouth.

Have you realized how much God must love you that he would use you as a vessel and a vehicle for his word? Do we ever stop as pastors to consider the awesome task we have? God does not call you to stand on Sunday morning and shoot from the hip. He does not ask you to spend all week thinking of stuff to say. He says: I'll place my words in your mouth; you just speak it. Have you thought about the awesome task we've been given: to stand as men and women of God with the Word of God in our mouths? God entrusts his word in my mouth.

God endangers his word to my mouth

Not only does he entrust his word to my mouth, he *endangers* his word to my mouth. God takes a risk when he puts his word in my mouth. He's gambling when he puts his word in my mouth.

God risks that I will taint his word with my weakness. First of all, he takes the risk that his word will be tainted when it comes through my life. He takes the risk that it will be tainted by my weaknesses, by the residue of sin in my life. He risks that his word would be tempered by my weaknesses, that I would not speak words of compassion through the bitterness of my experience. He risks that his word might not come through because of my fear. When I become obsessed and concerned and consumed by how the sheep will receive the word, I might back off and back up and not declare totally what God has given me. He takes a risk that I might see their faces and back up with fear. He takes a risk when he puts it in my life because of the weaknesses and the finitude of my humanity. He takes a risk that I will compromise his word. He takes a risk that I will be intimidated by those who would hear his word.

And yet he says: I put my word in your mouth.

God risks that I will claim that his words are my words. He takes a risk that once he puts his word in my mouth, the arrogance of my humanity would claim that his words are my words. That I would become the focal point. That I would imply that I'm the source. And yet he says it's his word in my mouth.

God risks that I will claim that my words are his words. He also takes a risk that I will make my word his word. God puts his word in my mouth, and he takes a risk that when I have been established as one with his word in my mouth, when I am recognized and affirmed as one who has his word in my mouth, I will then make my words his word.

His word never returns void but will always accomplish that for which it has been sent forth. His word never fails. The heavens may pass away and the mountains crumble, but his word will never pass away. His word is never wrong. So when I stand with his words in my mouth, when I speak his words through my mouth with my voice, then that which his word declares must be true. If I speak his word and declare that you are healed, if it's his word, you better be healed. When we imply our words are God's words and they do not come true, we leave behind a battlefield of broken and scarred people.

My son's godmother, Jean, several years ago had cancer. She had been in and out of the hospital, and after being very sick, she came to church one Sunday morning. And when Jean came to the service, there was a high time. The Spirit of the Lord was there. The anointing of the Lord was there. People were celebrating. They were rejoicing. Everyone was so glad to see Jean back.

And I stood in the midst of that celebration and that high, heavy anointing of the presence of God and I said, "Oh, praise the Lord that Jean is back today. Praise God." Everybody celebrated. And I said, "Jean, thus saith the Lord: God would have you know that your sickness is not unto death." All the saints celebrated. They rejoiced—Praise the Lord! Praise the Lord!— because the word of the Lord had come forth. And God had said: Your sickness is not unto death.

Three weeks later Jean died. My daughter came to me with tears in her eyes and said, "Daddy, what happened? You said that God told the church Auntie Jean wouldn't die. Daddy, what happened?" With tears in my eyes, I held my daughter and said, "Baby, Daddy was wrong."

When God puts his word in my mouth, he takes a risk that I will say my words and declare they are his words. How many times have we as pastors spoken out of the sincere desire to encourage, and yet we've made our words appear to be God's word? The body of Christ is in danger today, because words God has never spoken are being declared. And lives are being broken and crushed and disillusioned, because we're speaking our words and claiming them as his words.

God entrusts his word to your mouth, pastor. God sovereignly chose you as his holy mouthpiece. For reasons known only unto him, he chose you. And you stand before the people of God with his word in your mouth. You must never stand with intimidation. You must never back off of it. You must never twist it and turn it. You must never compromise it. You declare it, and you declare it with boldness, because when God puts his word in your mouth, he not only entrusts his word to you, he not only endangers his word, but he empowers his word. It's not you. It's the power of his word. He is looking for a mouthpiece, one who will submit to him and allow the power of his words to come forth. He is looking for someone who will speak the anointed word of God. God has loved you that much and chosen you that much that he would put his words in your mouth. Don't forget that.

It is a high and holy trust. It is a challenging trust. It is sometimes a frightful trust. But it is a demonstration of the very power of God, because when he speaks, things happen. When he speaks, sick folk get well, depressed folk get encouraged. When he speaks, salvation goes forth. There is power in his word.

God promises to bless his word. He never promised to bless my word about his word. For the degree to which I stand with his word in my mouth, I stand with the very creative and delivering and salvific power of God. You don't have to spend all week thinking of stuff to say; if you stay in the word of God, you won't have enough time to say it all. His word is what changes lives.

His word is what brings forth deliverance. His word is what lifts up bowed down heads. His word is what dries tear-stained eyes. His word is what saves families. His word is what brings back wayward children. His word is what encourages us as we walk along the way. It is the power of his word.

For God's word to be in your mouth, your life must be in his hand

So watch what God says: I place my word in your mouth. If you place your life in my hand, we can do something. By my sovereign will I have placed you. I may have set you before thirty. I may have set you before thousands. I may have set you before a Sunday school class. I may have set you in a one-on-one discipleship. But I have set you there because I put my words in your mouth. I have put my words in your mouth to touch and change lives. And you cannot change lives until you've been changed yourself by the power of the living God.

So, pastors, go forth realizing that you have his word in your mouth, and his word in your mouth can touch and change lives if your life is in his hand. His word, my mouth; my life, his hand. It's his word in my mouth, and my life in his hand. That's what makes the difference. It all depends on whose hand it's in. The difference in your life and my life depends on whose hand it's in. The difference in your ministry and the ministry that is ineffective is whose hand it's in. It's not about the numbers; it's about the anointing. It's not about the size; it's about the sovereign power of God. Because the thing that makes the difference is that you will speak his word in your mouth, and you will live your life in his hand, because it all depends on whose hand it's in.

A violin in my hand will get you some squeaky noise; but a violin in Itzhak Perlman's hand will get you the music of the masters. Marble in my hand is just a piece of ugly, dirt-covered stone; but marble in Michelangelo's hand will get you a magnificent *David*. A peanut in my hand is just a small snack; but a peanut in George Washington Carver's hand is peanut butter and shoe polish. A basketball in my hand is worth about $29.95; but a basketball in Kobe's hand and in LeBron's hand with hang time is worth about $30 million. A tennis racquet in my hand is a dangerous weapon; but a tennis racquet in the Williams sisters' hands is a tennis champion. A golf club in my hand means "look out, there's trouble coming"; but a golf club in Tiger Woods's hand is a Masters champion, because it all depends on whose hand it's in.

A rod in my hand may beat off the dogs; but a rod in Moses' hand will part the Red Seas of your life. The jawbone of an ass in my hand is the remains of a dead donkey; but a jawbone in Samson's hand will destroy the Philistines. A slingshot in my hand is a kid's toy; but a slingshot in David's hand will drop the Goliaths in your life, because it all depends on whose hand it's in.

Spit and clay in my hand will get you a little mud cake; but spit and clay in Jesus' hand will open blinded eyes. Two fish and five loaves of bread will get you a couple of fish sandwiches in my hand; but in Jesus' hand it will feed the five thousand. Nails in my hand might get you a little birdhouse; but nails in Jesus' hand hanging on the cross between two thieves on a hill called Calvary is salvation for the world, because it all depends on whose hand it's in.

You ought to take those hands and put them together and bless the Lord. Thank him that he's called you to be a pastor. Thank him that he's put his words in your mouth. Thank him that the anointing of God rests in your life. Thank him that he's picked you up and turned you around. Thank him that he's placed you before his people with his word in your mouth.

Kenneth Ulmer serves as the senior pastor-teacher of Faithful Central Bible Church in Inglewood, California.